D1563438

~ *Cultural Crusaders* ~

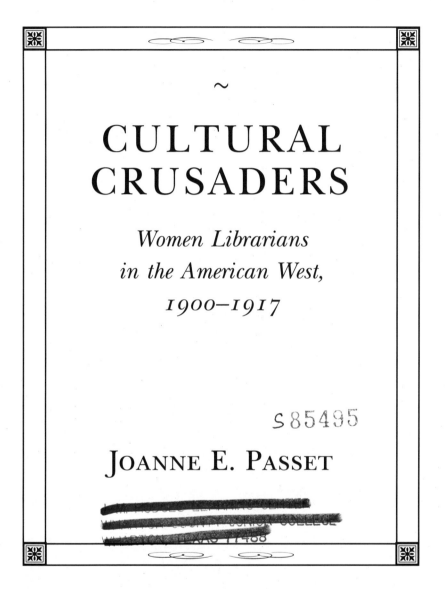

~

CULTURAL CRUSADERS

Women Librarians
in the American West,

1900–1917

JOANNE E. PASSET

UNIVERSITY OF NEW MEXICO PRESS
Albuquerque

Library of Congress Cataloging-in-Publication Data
Passet, Joanne Ellen.
Cultural crusaders : women librarians in the American
West, 1900–1917 / Joanne E. Passet.
—1st ed. p. cm. Includes bibliographical references and index.

ISBN No. 0–8263–1530–5
Contents: 1. Cultivating the "library spirit"—2. Who
was the western librarian?—3. Initial impressions — 4. In the
absence of other agencies—5. Bringing books and people together—
6. Creating the library habit—7. A professional watershed —
8. Four who served—Conclusion.

1. Women librarians—West (U.S.)—History—20th century. 2. Libraries—
West (U.S.)—History—20th century. I. Title.

Z682.4.W65P37 1994
020'.82—dc20
93–46764 CIP

Designed by Linda M. Tratechaud

~ *For Stephen* ~

~ *Contents* ~

~ *Acknowledgments* ~

Just as library school graduates went west in search of professional positions nearly one hundred years ago, I too went west for my first faculty position. My move from Bloomington, Indiana, to Los Angeles, California, seemed almost as adventurous as the experiences of those women who left family, friends, and all that was familiar in their quest for personal and professional development. As I traveled about the West in search of their records I came to love the arid New Mexico landscape, Colorado's snow-capped Rockies, and Washington's rolling wheat fields. I began to appreciate the loneliness and isolation, as well as the warm western hospitality, that these early western librarians had described.

It is impossible to undertake, let alone complete, a book of this nature without assistance from numerous sources. At Bluffton College, Bowling Green State University, and Indiana University I had the fortune to study with several historians who made a lasting impression on their student. These include Von Hardesty, James H. Madison, and Bernard Sternsher. I am especially indebted to the late John D. Unruh, Jr., an outstanding teacher and rigorous scholar who encouraged this student's interest in historical research and the American West.

David Nordloh, Jeanne Peterson, Bill Reese, and Jean Robinson, colleagues at Indiana University, have provided timely words of encouragement and advice. Gail Londergan, Deanna B. Marcum, and Wayne A. Wiegand gave generously of their time by reading and commenting on the manuscript. I also appreciate the interest Barbara Guth, my editor at the University of New Mexico Press, has shown in this project, and I have benefited from her suggestions. Many people have provided comments and advice, but any errors of fact and interpretation that remain in this text are mine alone.

Several agencies provided grants that enabled me to conduct extensive research travel to western archives, manuscript repositories, and libraries throughout the country. They are the National Endowment for the Humanities, the American Association for State and Local

History, the Academic Senate Committee on Research at the University of California, Los Angeles, and the Office of University Research and Graduate Development at Indiana University. I also am grateful to the Research Development Committee of the School of Library and Information Science at Indiana University for providing me with release time from teaching during the spring semester 1992.

Numerous archivists and librarians facilitated my use of many archival and manuscript collections and encouraged my work on this topic. I would like to extend my appreciation to Terry Abraham, Ron Baker, Kerry Bartels, Tim Blevins, Maynard Brichford, Cindy L. Brown, Frank Cook, Steven Fisher, Richard S. Hobbs, Carol Lichtenberg, Betty Lloyd, Linda Long, Sarah Long, Mervin Mecklenburg, Karen McWilliams, Larin Metzer, John Newman, Jean Nudd, Carol Silvers, Cindy Swanson, and Thomas Wilsted. I also would like to acknowledge the courteous assistance of librarians at the University of Arizona, Colorado State University, the Denver Public Library Western History Department, the Spokane Public Library, Stanford University, the State Historical Society of Wisconsin, and the University of California, Los Angeles.

Gardner Hanks and Charles Bolles, of the Idaho State Library; Mary Ginnane, of the Oregon State Library; and Christine Hamilton-Pennell, of the Colorado Department of Education, provided me with several opportunities to combine speaking engagements with research travel—I treasure my memories of their friendship and hospitality. I also am deeply grateful to the interlibrary loan staffs at the UCLA University Research Library and the Indiana University Libraries for locating many obscure documents quickly and efficiently.

Damiana Chavez (UCLA) and Beverly Killion (Indiana) provided valuable assistance with grant administration, and several graduate assistants made it possible for me to work more efficiently. They include Kuang Pei Tu, Sue Davies, and Patty Schafer at UCLA; Nola Hull, Beth Blakesley, and Jennifer Bauman at Indiana University. I also appreciate my students' interest in and enthusiasm for this project during the past five years, in particular, Sandy Garcia-Myers, Nancy Godleski, and Debra J. Oswald have reminded me of the importance of leading a balanced life.

Friends and family sustain the researcher by providing advice, support and encouragement throughout a long project. I am indebted to Mary Niles Maack, my coauthor on another research project, for her sage advice, confidence in my abilities, and warm friendship. She has taught me what mentoring is all about. While it is impossible to name everyone who has provided encouragement, I also would like to thank my friends, Sarah Cooper, Liz Gnerre, Nancy Lair, Tom Munson, and Dale Treleven; my family, Norman and Almeda Passet, Gerald and Darlene Wolter; and my husband, Stephen G. Wolter, who has made countless sacrifices to accommodate my research and career.

~ *Introduction* ~

Many myths exist about librarians and about the American West. Prevailing images—cultivated in scholarly writing as well as in popular culture—depict the West as predominantly "masculine" and the librarian as a mild-mannered bearer of culture, a gentle tamer.[1] Western library development coincided with the growing availability of professionally trained librarians, most of whom were women, from eastern and midwestern states. Like many late-nineteenth- and early-twentieth-century Americans, library school graduates regarded the West, with its newly established libraries and library commissions, as a fertile field for their work, an outlet for their missionary zeal, and a place where they could develop as independent women.

Coming of age in an era that included the rise of the women's club movement, heightened interest in social reform, and expanding educational opportunities, these late-nineteenth-century women entered what rapidly became a female-intensive profession during its formative years. The American Library Association was organized in 1876, and Melvil Dewey opened the first School of Library Economy at Columbia College (later Columbia University) in 1887. Librarianship represented an accessible occupation for the educated woman who desired both to improve society and to be self-sufficient. As librarianship professionalized and rapidly feminized, it also shifted from a collection-oriented to a client-oriented field. Thus, for at least a brief time, many of these early librarians found their personal and professional goals in harmony. Indeed, historians have referred to the period 1887–1917 as a "Golden Age" in library development.

Fueled by their desire to connect books and readers, western librarians sought to share their cherished Anglo-American canon with a diverse western readership that included rural and urban residents, children and adults, working- and middle-class men and women, immigrants, Native Americans, and African Americans. These predominantly middle-class, white, librarians' interactions with other racial and ethnic groups are discussed when adequate documentation permits.[2]

Motivated by a "library spirit" instilled during their professional training, these women both embodied and challenged contemporary gender ideology. Although they transcended the Victorian image of woman when they moved into the public arena to deliver speeches, engaged in community politics, and used their powers of persuasion to extend library service, these women continued to be influenced by the family, a potent factor shaping the direction of their lives. According to LeeAnne G. Kryder, however, the family influence ultimately diminished as the Progressive Era woman began to place growing emphasis on individual interests.[3] Although many of her activities did benefit society, the "New Woman" increasingly found herself in situations that promoted personal development.

The pioneering phase of western library work began to wane during the second decade of the twentieth century. Wayne A. Wiegand argues that 1917 marks a watershed in American library history because it represents the conclusion of a period of rapid expansion, strong leadership, and development of new services.[4] Moreover, American society increasingly emphasized the individual, upward mobility, and consumerism, and educated women discovered that "the social context of their lives contained little to sustain their idealism and enthusiasm."[5] Librarians, along with many others, became disillusioned. By the end of World War I, library salaries lagged and librarians no longer seemed to possess a shared sense of purpose. Instead, their altruistic vision of service and their sense of mission appears to have disappeared into the crosscurrents of American history.

The convergence of women, a new profession, and the early-twentieth-century American West provides a context in which to ask several questions. Although recent scholarship has enhanced our understanding of the lives of women homesteaders, teachers, and prostitutes, much remains to be known about single working women in the American West.[6] A number of works have explored the single woman's role in turn-of-the-century America, but primarily in the urban context. Joanne Meyerowitz provides a fascinating exploration of the lives of thousands of female clerks, saleswomen, teachers, nurses, and others who lived apart from their families in Chicago, while Kathy Peiss examines working women's leisure-time activities in New York.[7]

A goal of this study is to contribute to our understanding of how one group of women—librarians— constructed and gave meaning to their lives as independent women in predominantly rural western communities. Did they view library work in the West as an opportunity for advancement, or were they motivated primarily by altruistic impulses? To what extent did they attempt to re-create familial or female subcultures in western communities? Did they ultimately break the patriarchal family claim and challenge contemporary gender stereotypes, or did life as single women in western communities reinforce societal conventions and parental expectations?

This study also seeks to expand our understanding of the woman's role in western community building. A body of research has begun to address the work of western women's clubs in the establishment of libraries, but little is known about the librarians who carried their efforts forward.[8] Although these librarians often worked in geographically isolated communities, they retained a strong sense of connectedness to other parts of the nation. To what extent were they touched by the western environment? Were they cultural imperialists, trying to impose the gospel of libraries according to eastern and midwestern library leaders, or did they transform their knowledge of library work when they encountered the West? And did this sense of connectedness inhibit or promote cultural innovation?

Finally, this study attempts to place women at the center of the history of library development. It is ironic that the published history of this female-intensive profession is "largely a history of men, often directors of large libraries, [written] by men."[9] Women, and the areas in which they participated—in particular, children's work and cataloging—are significantly underrepresented, even ignored. Dee Garrison further obscures women's contributions to librarianship by suggesting that they stunted the development of librarianship as a profession and consequently shaped the inferior status of the public library as a cultural institution. Such an approach oversimplifies a very complex issue. Moreover, she does not clearly distinguish between the many amateurs who worked in libraries and professionally trained librarians.[10]

Suzanne Hildenbrand argues that as it upgraded requirements and expanded, the library profession became more accessible to middle-class women while less-advantaged men dropped out because they could no longer afford the increasing "opportunity costs."[11] Instead of stunting the profession's development, Hildenbrand proposes that feminization produced a golden age, one in which women transformed passive repositories of books into dynamic cultural and educational institutions. The experience of the early professional librarians who pioneered in western library work lends support to this thesis.

For a number of years I have been deeply interested in the lives of early women librarians—not only the few who achieved national recognition, but also the hundreds of unremembered women who entered this field during its formative years. A few professionally trained female librarians worked in the West before 1900, but the majority arrived after the turn of the century. They are the focus of this study. I identified the names of 311 professionally trained women who worked as librarians in the West between 1900 and 1917 (the year identified by Wiegand as a professional watershed) by examining contemporary journal literature, library school catalogs, alumni registers, and biographical directories.[12] Public, academic, school, and special/governmental libraries are represented. Although I attempted to be comprehensive, this number most certainly underrepresents the total population because names were omitted if data were incomplete (it sometimes became difficult to trace women who married) or if the specific location and dates of western employment could not be verified. The emphasis of this study is on library school women, but it also considers contributions of several men and untrained women who devoted their lives to western library work.

Because library development occurred on a statewide basis, this study utilizes a definition of the West that includes the eleven states west of the one-hundredth meridian. They are Arizona, California, Colorado, Idaho, Montana, Nevada, New Mexico, Oregon, Utah, Washington, and Wyoming. Support for libraries spread more rapidly in Colorado and the Pacific Coast states than it did in Arizona, Nevada, New Mexico, Utah, and Wyoming, with their vast expanses of desert and sparse population. Readers should remember that this study focuses more on the women—their impressions of the West, changing personal and professional aspirations, and progress—than it does on the institutions where they were employed. An extensive history of western libraries and librarianship remains to be written.

A major challenge to the writing of western women's history is the location of primary sources. Although most of the women who worked as western librarians were single, had no children, and are long forgotten, some of their words have survived. Conscious of their status as pioneers, they corresponded regularly with library school directors, faculty, colleagues, and friends. These letters, located in alumni files at several universities, contain reactions to a new environment, descriptions of their daily lives, impressions of people and institutions, and insight into the ways that they, as independent working women, came to terms with the West. Moreover, the emotional bond that developed between the library school directors and a number of their students fostered trust and confidences. Although some self-censorship undoubtedly occurred as these women wrote, the items they chose to include in and exclude from their correspondence provides an indication of those experiences that made significant impressions on them.

Additional materials—personal papers, institutional archives, correspondence of prominent librarians (including state librarians, directors of library schools, and secretaries of state library commissions), correspondence of state officials (governors, secretaries of state), publications of state governments, and the Carnegie Corporation library correspondence—provide a rich, if widely dispersed, base of primary evidence. These materials have been supplemented by such printed sources as annual reports, local histories, institutional histories, alumni registers, biographical directories, city directories, and contemporary local newspapers. Photographs provide yet another view of western women librarians, and have been chosen to depict the women and their varied environments. We are fortunate that Mabel Wilkinson documented her written account of travels in Wyoming with photographs. Several of these truly invaluable images are reprinted in this volume.

It was in the early library schools that these western librarians acquired their deeply rooted commitment to public service. The eastern and midwestern schools from which they graduated include the New York State Library School (founded in 1887 at Columbia College and moved to the New York State Library, Albany, in 1889), Pratt Institute Library School (1890), Drexel Institute Library School (1892), the University of Illinois Library School (founded in 1893 at Armour Institute of Technology and moved to the University of Illinois in 1897), the Training School for Children's Librarians in Pittsburgh (1901), Simmons College Library School (1902), the Western Reserve University Library School (1904), the Indiana Library School (1905), the Wisconsin Library School (1906), and the New York Public Library School (1912). No graduates of the Carnegie Library School in Atlanta and the Syracuse University Library School are represented in this population.

The turn-of-the-century West offered few educational opportunities for local men and women who wished to prepare for careers in librarianship. Several public libraries conducted training classes, but graduates usually expected to join the host institution's staff upon completion of the course. The Los Angeles Public Library (1891) and the Denver Public Library (1893) conducted such classes at an early date, but many other classes flourished during this era. These programs initially trained prospective employees, but eventually their graduates exceeded the number of positions available locally and began looking elsewhere for employment. Summer schools for librarians, sponsored by state library commissions or by academic institutions, enabled untrained librarians to take affordable courses during their summer vacations without jeopardizing their positions.[13]

Aside from public library training classes and summer library schools, the West had no professional education for librarians until 1911 when William E. Henry established a program at the University of Washington. Graduating its first class of ten students in 1913, the Washington school sought to educate librarians for that institution and for libraries within the state. Consequently, it did not provide significant numbers of librarians for other western states, with the possible exception of Oregon, during its early years.[14]

In 1913 the Riverside Public Library began its School of Library Service, and a year later the Los Angeles Public Library converted its training class into a full-scale library school. The University of California offered a six-week summer school course in library methods as early as 1902, but did not conduct it again until 1906. After that year, the university offered the course sporadically until 1918, at which time it instituted a year-long program in library science.

Stereotypes, of librarians and of western women, will persist until more of their voices are heard. The following chapters document the personal and professional lives of several hundred women who participated in the development and diffusion of one cultural institution, the library, in the American West. As we listen to their voices, excerpted from correspondence and journals, we learn about the reality of their environment, their motivations, aspirations, frustrations, and accomplishments. Chapter 1, "Cultivating the 'Library Spirit,'" examines the context in which these women studied and worked. In Chapter 2, "Who Was the Western Librarian?," a clearer picture of these women's social, cultural, and economic background emerges. Chapter 3 documents their initial impressions of western communities, institutions, and people. Chapters 4, 5, and 6 focus on their efforts to extend the influence of academic and public libraries in the West. Chapter 7 considers the extent to which 1917 represents a turning point in the history of the profession and in the lives of these western women librarians. Finally, Chapter 8 contains minibiographies of four representative women who embody the spirit of the cultural crusaders.

~ one ~

Cultivating the "Library Spirit"

Professionally trained librarians were not available to staff the nation's libraries until 1887, when Melvil Dewey opened his School of Library Economy at Columbia College. During the next three decades over a dozen additional schools came into existence, but none appeared in the West until the second decade of the twentieth century. It was in these early schools, with their intensity and strong sense of community, that the cultural crusaders acquired a deeply rooted commitment to public service.

From the beginning, Dewey promoted library work as a vocation especially suited to college women. Women's presence on the campuses of normal schools, colleges, and universities had increased from 21 percent in 1870 to nearly 50 percent by 1920.[1] After graduating from college, however, many experienced a crisis—would they marry, return home, or find work? While the typical life pattern continued to include marriage and motherhood, late-nineteenth-century families began to acknowledge that their daughters would experience an interval between the attainment of adulthood and marriage. Teaching, one of the few fields accessible to educated women, became a stage in the life cycle for many American women.[2] Such helping professions as nursing, librarianship, and social work also welcomed them.

Mary E. Ahern, editor of *Public Libraries,* one of the library profession's earliest journals, was quick to recognize librarianship as a viable alternative for the growing numbers of women "in the labor market today, involuntarily or otherwise."[3] Most early library schools required only a high school diploma or its equivalent and an entrance examination for admission. As a result, library school came to represent an attractive option to both college graduates and women who, for a variety of reasons, lacked bachelor's degrees.

Such popular periodicals as *The Dial, Ladies Home Journal,* and *World's Work* also promoted librarianship as an ideal occupation for the educated woman who wished to make a positive contribution to society. An article in the February 1900 issue of the *Ladies Home Journal,* entitled "What It Means to be a Librarian," prompted women throughout the country to request application materials from the nation's library schools. Mary E. Hazeltine, preceptress of the Wisconsin Library School, reported:

> The *Ladies Home Journal* for the current month also struck Wisconsin!! . . . I presume that every mail from this time on until I land in the lunatic asylum will be followed up with similar requests.[4]

This and other articles promoted library work as a form of educational service analogous to teaching. Authors of such articles acknowledged that librarians received only nominal compensation for their labors, but appealed to the Progressive-era woman's desire to bring about better social and moral conditions. Indeed, women flocked to library schools, and between 1888 and 1921 approximately 94 percent of the forty-five hundred graduates who emerged were female.

Enthusiasm and zeal characterize most new movements or professions, and librarianship was no exception.[5] Even though from its inception the curriculum of the nation's first library school was technical, graduates emerged infused by what they came to call the "library spirit." Dewey's preoccupation with efficiency should not obscure his belief that a properly functioning library enabled librarians to accomplish a greater mission for society.

Because many early library schools depended on frequent guest lecturers, students had ample exposure to inspirational practitioners who exemplified the library spirit in action. Indeed, many librarians acknowledged "that [the] indefinable something we called the 'library spirit'" provided them with a common, noble goal and a sense of cohesion. Although library school directors seldom discussed "library spirit" formally, they were concerned if their students did not seem to possess it. When faculty at the Wisconsin Library School perceived that a student's "spirit was not right," they required her to report to the preceptress for a talk. It was this "spirit" that "accounts for much of the cohesion and driving force of the modern library movement."[6]

Most library school directors attempted to foster an esprit de corps among their students, connecting them not only to one another, but also to those who preceded them and to those who would follow. Mary E. Hazeltine encouraged her students at the Wisconsin Library School to participate in a variety of recreational and cultural activities outside the lecture hall. Hazeltine and other library school directors believed that such participation not only revitalized hard-working students, but also contributed to the development of a corporate spirit.

Additionally, library school directors established and perpetuated a number of school customs designed to promote continuity and a sense of loyalty among alumni. These included class parties, class letters written by graduates to new students, a May Day celebration where alumni and guests could mingle with students, and a closing convocation exercise, where alumni and faculty welcomed students to the profession.[7] Schools also sponsored class trips and began alumni reunions at state and national library association meetings. This sense of connectedness sustained many librarians when they reached the West.

A growing body of literature suggests that western life did not liberate women from traditional gender roles, and that they discarded them reluctantly only after the roles became too difficult to maintain.[8] Richard White refers to the unmarried women who worked as teachers, seamstresses, laundry workers, and domestic servants, positions that did not challenge the female sphere's traditional boundaries.[9] Glenda Riley's comparative study of women settlers on the prairie and the plains lends further support to the thesis that western women's lives were more influenced "by gender considerations than by region."[10] Indeed, the example of these librarians does not raise questions about the influence of gender on their lives, but it does demonstrate how they used gender expectations to their advantage.

Working within gender constraints did not prevent western women from assuming active roles as "civilizers." Elizabeth Jameson encourages historians to avoid the gentle tamer/civilizer dichotomy, and to focus instead on the fact that women "created a female community that supported them and they helped to shape communities and politics in the west."[11] Thus, women are active participants, and not passive objects, in western history. Research on women teachers, in particular, illustrates women's contributions to western community life. Mary Hurlbut Cordier's study of schoolwomen in Iowa, Kansas, and Nebraska from the 1860s to 1920s documents how their work "propelled them into public roles that stretched the limitations of gender."[12] Only a few articles, book chapters, and biographical sketches address the western woman librarian's role as a civilizing influence. Most of these, however, focus on the experiences of exemplars—without considering questions of gender and region.[13]

Historians have devoted considerable attention to working-class women, but only a few have examined the experiences of middle-class women and their efforts to enter the professional work force.[14] Additionally, these studies tend to emphasize the negative aspects of feminization, obscuring other aspects of a professional woman's life. Nancy F. Cott argues convincingly that women's advances in higher education—specifically college teaching—can be attributed more to "large-scale economic and labor market conditions and to factors within each profession . . . than to the state of organized feminism."[15] The number of women in male-dominated professions, as opposed to those in female-intensive occupations, supports this thesis. While by 1910 only 1 percent of all lawyers and 6 percent of all physicians were women, approximately 52 percent of social workers, 79 percent of librarians, and 93 percent of professional nurses were female.[16] Meanwhile, opportunities also developed for women in department stores and offices, where they began to replace men as clerks, but supervisory and administrative positions there remained elusive.[17]

Women who tried to enter such "masculine" fields as science and medicine encountered significant resistance. According to Margaret Rossiter, those who attempted to enter science experienced topical and hierarchical segregation, the former when they found themselves limited to work in such feminine areas as home economics and hygiene, the latter when they became lab assistants under male supervision. While they made minimal progress in traditional, or male-dominated professions, women moved with greater ease into occupations that depended on a cheap source of labor and appeared to be compatible with feminine talents.[18] Even after they acquired the appropriate credentials, however, late-nineteenth- and early-twentieth-century women discovered that amateurs had a firm hold on many positions. Susan Reverby's study of nursing reveals the existence of a schism that developed during the late nineteenth century between professionally trained women and scores of apprentices. The situation worsened as hospitals failed to employ their own nursing students (the first hospital school of nursing opened in 1873). Moreover, some nurses resisted professionalization, maintaining the belief that feminine character, and not specialized knowledge, qualified women to become nurses.[19]

Like their counterparts in nursing, graduate librarians soon learned that library school certificates did not guarantee employment. Although thousands of libraries came into existence in America during the late nineteenth century, most, in their infancy, were tiny, underfunded, and open only a few hours each week. For a number of years, small communities persisted in the practice of appointing untrained residents as librarians, in part because library boards wanted to economize, but also because they viewed the librarian's position as a form of charity—an honorable means of assisting needy men and women in the community. In 1891 Caroline Hewins observed that "many inefficient middle-aged women [were] in libraries, who were put there because they had no means of support."[20]

Library board members often expressed a preference for local women, believing that they could be more easily controlled than "foreign" (nonlocal) library school graduates. Several additional factors, among them limited financial support for libraries, contributed to this tendency to hire part-time and amateur local librarians. Board members justified paying local women less because they could live at home and would not have travel expenses. The practice was not confined to small town, one-person libraries. In larger institutions, untrained library directors, especially men, also expressed reservations about imported librarians. Los Angeles librarian Charles Lummis feared that the technical knowledge of eastern library school graduates could "overshadow our knowledge of our own needs." It is possible that Lummis, a self-made librarian, may have felt threatened by the advent of trained women who could compete for his position.[21]

The public only gradually accepted the need for librarians with professional training. Even some professional leaders, as late as 1905, claimed that native ability, liberal education, and broad culture resulted in a better librarian than did special professional education.[22] Eventually, however, it became evident that a systematic form of instruction promoted efficiency and professional pride while at the same time meeting the growing demand for public library workers. And although amateurs could develop technical proficiency, they seldom possessed the professionally trained librarian's broader vision of librarianship and network of professional contacts.

As library work professionalized, boards of trustees began to hire professional librarians, if only on a temporary basis, to organize their collections. The scarcity of full-time library positions led many early graduates to accept these temporary positions, which took them throughout the country. At each stop they organized the library's collections, and they often trained a local woman who would continue the work after the librarian's departure. A number of library school graduates enjoyed itinerant work because it provided them with a measure of flexibility and an opportunity to see different regions. In 1903 a traveling library organizer named Mary Robbins concluded that people "in good health, with a fondness for travel and the study of human nature" would enjoy the work.[23] Even those who enjoyed travel, however, hoped that itinerant positions ultimately would lead to full-time appointments:

> I have thought that if nothing of a permanent nature comes
> up I would be glad to do more organizing and thus in
> taking one or two temporary positions perhaps work into
> something permanent.[24]

It was through such work, then, that a number of graduate librarians had their first exposure to the West.

Turn-of-the-century librarians encountered a West that was becoming increasingly urban, but in 1900 only four cities—Denver, Los Angeles, Salt Lake City, and San Francisco—had populations of one hundred thousand or greater. Portland and Seattle followed close behind. Arid and mountainous areas developed more slowly.[25] Like many Americans, these librarians expected to earn higher wages in the West. Even with the higher cost of living, western workers usually earned higher real wages.[26] Western expansion was geographically uneven, but overall the region surpassed the national rate of urbanization between 1890 and 1920 as it grew in population from 3 to 9 million. Nonetheless, the West's vastness meant that many areas remained overwhelmingly rural, with economies based on lumber, mining, and agriculture.

Environmental conditions—distance, sparse settlement, and geographic barriers—made it difficult to arouse and sustain interest in libraries. Western communities, of necessity, focused their attention on such basic activities as the organization of state and local governments, securing water supplies and sewage systems, and on such civic improvements as courthouses, jails, and paved streets. Charles Lummis's 1905 description of Los Angeles could have applied to a number of western communities: "This city . . . is strained by its endeavor to be Born Grown Up—in other words, to provide in ten years the civic advantages which Eastern cities have required a century to attain."[27]

Even though community residents wished to establish churches, schools, and libraries, a small population base, geographic dispersion, poor economy and tax base, and climate conducive to outdoor life retarded developments in many areas. With only 6 percent of the nation's libraries in 1875, western residents had limited access to books. Concentrated on the West Coast, these existing libraries included social, society, academic, government, quasi-military, commercial circulating, and specialized collections of religious, agricultural, and legal works. In an 1896 report that excluded California, Oregon, and Washington (states where library development was the most advanced), Denver librarian John Cotton Dana identified only seventeen "public" libraries with five thousand or more volumes in the West. Many of these, however, exited in state capitols and at state universities, relatively inaccessible to the general public.[28]

A few years later, another Colorado librarian observed that "the number of towns in the West which are large enough to maintain a library is small and very few of them contain libraries or seem interested in the work." A report focusing on California libraries, issued in 1902, indicated that fewer than half of that state's 120 incorporated towns and cities had public libraries, and that book stores and reading rooms were infrequent. And when Seattle librarian Charles W. Smith attempted to compile a list of public libraries in the Northwest in 1905, he found only forty-four supported by public taxation—four in Idaho, fourteen in Montana, four in Oregon, sixteen in Washington, and six in Wyoming.[29] Clearly, library work was in its infancy.

While some pioneers on the western frontier hungered for books, public sentiment about libraries for the most part appeared to be "inert, apathetic, profoundly indifferent," and library workers observed that the cause seemed "to have few friends who believe that it is the birthright of every boy and girl." They attributed this apathy to the nature of western residents, many of whom had migrated there "from pure love of adventure" or "in search of health." Others had "been very largely attracted by the hope of making a fortune rapidly in mining, or stock raising, or in railroad and irrigation enterprises," or because they wished "to take part in the unusual activity of a new country." Even after abandoning their dreams, the feeling that "this is just a place to be patched up and made temporarily livable" persisted. As late as 1919, the preceptress of the Wisconsin Library School observed that

> as we go further west, it is evident that libraries need more attention, just plain every day things done to them. . . . All the frills we have put on to them in the east and middle west can not yet be attempted in many parts of the west, because the fundamental things have not yet been accomplished.[30]

Thus, the region had a few large libraries, but the reality for most smaller communities consisted of a meager collection of books, often established under the auspices of private philanthropy, especially women's clubs.

Once western women had survived the hardships of pioneer days, they sought to provide their children with some of the advantages they had known back east. Eastern women's clubs tended to arise out of an interest in self-improvement, but their western counterparts frequently gave as their primary reason for existence the establishment of a community library. A few—the Ladies Literary Club of Salt Lake City, the Woman's Club of Olympia, Washington, and the Ebell Society of Oakland, California—organized as early as the 1870s and 1880s, but the majority of western women's clubs came into existence after 1890.[31]

Initially established as organizations devoted to social activities, mutual interest in reading, and a desire for self-improvement, women's clubs provided an opportunity for their members to develop skills in public speaking, leadership, and organization. Growing concern about the impact of industrialization, immigration, and urbanization upon society led club women to shift their focus from cultural pursuits to educational and social reform activities. A 1912 report of the Butte Woman's Club exemplifies women's desire to make culture useful, noting that "it has thrown off the selfish idea of meeting to study this and that for personal improvements . . . and has become interested in service to the public." Jane C. Croly's 1898 history of women's clubs cites numerous instances of women who organized for the purpose of

1.1. King's Daughters Library, Monte Vista, Colorado, ca. 1890s.
Courtesy Denver Public Library, Western History Department

establishing a community library. Croly describes western women's efforts as especially meaningful in a place "lacking everything" where an "environment had to be created."[32]

Gaining confidence in their power to exert influence on the public sphere, club women campaigned on behalf of pure milk, the prevention of industrial pollution, and the establishment of kindergartens, public libraries, and state library commissions. According to Sophonisba P. Breckinridge, writing in 1933, women's clubs had a role in the establishment of approximately 75 percent of the nation's public libraries in existence at that time. One explanation for this substantial role in the library movement may be found in Karen J. Blair's work. She concludes that the formation of the General Federation of Women's Clubs in 1890, and the subsequent development of many state and regional federations, "formalized the right of women to turn their attention to civic work."[33]

Utah club women were second in the nation to federate, preceded only by Maine. Supporting a variety of projects—among them school lunches, the teaching of home economics, and physical education for women—they developed a traveling library system, and a number of local clubs in larger communities established libraries that they eventually turned over to their communities. Montana club women federated in 1904, and that same year began a small system of traveling libraries, reporting twenty in circulation by 1909. While Arizona would not have a traveling library system until much later, the Arizona Federation of Women's Clubs, organized in 1901, reported that thirty-seven clubs had established or sponsored libraries.

In several states, club women worked to develop state commissions that could oversee the work of traveling libraries or the development of public libraries. By 1899, the Woman's Columbian Club of Boise, Idaho, had fifteen traveling libraries—approximately eight hundred volumes—circulating throughout a state that had only one tax-supported public library by 1901. In 1900 it mounted a campaign for a state library commission, which included circular letters urging newly elected legislators, newspaper editors, public school officials, and teachers to endorse library legislation. The club women also exerted their influence on legislation by attending sessions of the state legislature en masse. Their efforts resulted in the establishment of the Idaho Free Library Commission in 1901, and a six-thousand-dollar appropriation. Oregon had no public libraries in 1899 when club women there federated, and they chose as one of their first projects to campaign for legislation to establish a library system. Nevada club women federated much later, in 1912. Perhaps because their state was so sparsely populated and could not realistically support libraries, they focused initially on raising money for scholarships, a home for delinquent boys, and conservation concerns, before turning their attention to public libraries.[34]

Club women regarded libraries as desirable for many reasons, first and foremost because they added a measure of stability to communities and gave them an impetus in the "right direction." According to Richard White, a key factor in the development of the West is that Anglo-American migrants essentially replicated eastern social and economic structures in order to guarantee their personal betterment.[35] While they came from a variety of backgrounds, club women tended to represent a community's elite. A librarian visiting Monterey, California, described the members of the Monterey Library Association as the "absolute rulers" of that town's social world. In other western communities, however, club women sometimes attributed class distinctions more to educational advantages than to financial status. Whatever the basis for their authority, they united with their husbands—civic leaders, merchants, educators, and the clergy—to help forge a community identity through problem solving.[36] The library represented one means by which they could enhance community life and ensure social order.

Club women in Modesto, California, hoped to keep boys out of the saloons by opening a poolroom with the public library as a minor feature in the corner. Everywhere, they seemed motivated by a positive power that they attributed to books and libraries. A Council, Idaho, woman indicated a willingness to give her house "and half my time . . . to organize a library club. I love the work because I know the good it does."[37]

Unfortunately, club women were not immune to conflict. A Tucumcari, New Mexico, woman, discouraged by the factionalism that she observed among the women in her community, lamented: "You would not believe that women who call themselves ladies could show such a narrow jealous spirit as many have since I began my campaigning." She was assured by a member of the Wisconsin Free Library Commission that the existence of these very conditions testified to her community's need for a library: "It is but additional evidence that an institution such as you propose is very much needed in your community."[38]

Once a club decided to establish a library, members usually began to collect books, employing a variety of methods. The Santa Fe Woman's Board of Trade held book showers and entertainments to which the admission fee was a book, while members of the Albuquerque Public Library Association appealed to the territorial governor for support.[39] Similar events were replicated throughout the West and collections grew slowly and haphazardly. Concern for quantity dominated concern for quality, and club women accepted many gifts that had been discarded from personal libraries because they were either worn from heavy use, or uninteresting.

Handicapped by tiny collections, limited funds, inadequate facilities, enormous distances, and thinly populated settlements, women's clubs struggled to provide the rudiments of library service. Members of the Current Events Club of Alamosa, Colorado, "volunteered their services as librarians, keeping the reading room open every afternoon from two to five and every evening except Sunday."[40] Some women,

1.2. Mrs. G. R. Miles, librarian of the Idaho Falls Public Library, 1908.
Courtesy Idaho State Historical Society

motivated by a desire to manage their collections more efficiently, enrolled in summer library schools. They also campaigned for library legislation to establish the work on a more permanent basis. Many housed collections in their club or meeting rooms until dedicated sites could be secured in more publicly accessible locations. Envisioning their libraries as places where the farmer's wife could rest when she came to town, where children could gather, and idle men could go instead of to saloons, they recognized the necessity of an attractive, central location.

In some western communities the library movement failed when initial enthusiasm waned, factionalism persisted, or a founder passed away. Libraries, begun with good intentions, were not updated and the books, once read, began to collect dust on the shelves. A librarian who visited Placerville, California, in 1905, discovered an abandoned library in the city hall that had been "established way back in Noah's time," while in another community she found three hundred volumes locked in a closet where only "a clairvoyant or [a] mind reader" would

1.3. Hayward, California, Carnegie Library, ca. 1907.
Courtesy American Library Association Archives

have been able to find them.[41] The failure of these libraries, unfortunately, led some residents to oppose the development of a public library, believing that it would share the same fate.

The passage of enabling laws facilitated local initiatives by providing for public support of libraries, and seven western states enacted such legislation between 1872 and 1896.[42] The availability of Andrew Carnegie's grants for library buildings further stimulated interest in libraries. Between 1899 and 1919, 280 communities in eleven western states received Carnegie library building grants (see Table 1.1). Nearly one third of these communities had no library prior to Carnegie's gift. These grants made it possible for many cities and towns to establish libraries on a more permanent basis, requiring as they did the community's commitment to provide support each year in the amount equal to 10 percent of the original Carnegie grant.

Club women often spearheaded the movement to apply for Carnegie money, but in some areas they encountered problems because they had not first carefully considered why the community needed a library building and what it would accomplish. Community leaders

Table 1.1 Western Communities Receiving Carnegie Library Building
Grants, 1899–1919

State	Range of Years that Grants Were Given	Numbers Given/ Communities with Previous Libraries
California	1899–1917	121/93
Washington	1901–1916	33/18
Colorado	1901–1917	27/18
Oregon	1901–1915	25/17
Utah	1903–1919	23/17
Montana	1901–1918	17/12
Wyoming	1899–1917	16/7
Idaho	1903–1914	10/6
Arizona	1899–1917	4/2
New Mexico	1902–1903	3/0
Nevada	1902	1/0
Total	1899–1919	280/190

Source: George Bobinski, *Carnegie Libraries* (Chicago: American Library Association, 1969).

sometimes viewed Carnegie grants as a way to obtain facilities for other activities. The citizens of Fort Benton, Montana, for example, planned to include a gymnasium in the library. Carnegie refused to fund this and similar requests for libraries that would house bowling alleys, museums, art galleries, and club rooms. While many communities did benefit from Carnegie money, it became a point of contention in others. A librarian visiting Salinas, California, described the factions she observed there as "saloon and anti-saloon; Carnegie and anti-Carnegie; and a dozen more."[43]

Club women provided the energy, dedication, and support that made it possible for western public libraries to spread and flourish, but as the years passed they also developed a variety of other reform interests. Thus, as libraries became more permanent features of their communities, they began to relinquish control.

When members of the American Library Association gathered in Portland, Oregon, for their 1905 annual meeting, they found western library work still in its infancy. The association had not met west of the Rocky Mountains since 1891, and western librarians hoped that a national meeting would provide the much-needed impetus to carry their efforts forward. In spite of the tireless efforts of the many club women who "nobly" upheld "the cause of the larger intellectual life" on the frontier, most library work remained in the hands of novices or self-made librarians.[44] The West made a deep impression on many attendees, who returned home convinced that it represented an opportunity for them to promote public happiness and democracy in a region where great wealth had not yet chilled the heart and governments were relatively pure.

~ two ~

Who Was the Western Librarian?

<blockquote>
~

SHE IS A WOMAN OF CULTURE AND REFINEMENT AND HAS AN *UPLIFTING* INFLUENCE. SHE BUBBLES OVER WITH LIFE AND ENTHUSIASM AND IS A BORN LEADER.

—*KATHARINE L. SHARP, 1906*
</blockquote>

Her name was Mary, Helen, Elizabeth, or Mabel. The daughter of a middle-class family, she was born in a midwestern state during the last half of the nineteenth century. She attended college, but did not always graduate. Remaining single, she chose to enter library school during her mid-to-late twenties because the profession appeared receptive to women, the work seemed compatible with her recently acquired education, and it provided an outlet for her social reform impulses. Prior to becoming a librarian she worked as a teacher, clerk, or library assistant, often in her home town. Although her work made it possible for her to be financially independent, she nonetheless remained devoted to her family and subject to its influence.

More than half of the western librarians for whom birthplace is known hailed from the Central United States, especially the states of Illinois, Iowa, and Ohio. Even so, birthplaces ranged from Maine to California and from Florida to Washington. The northeastern states accounted for smaller numbers of women (12.5 percent) and even fewer (2 percent) came from the Southeast (see Table 2.1). Before the establishment of library schools in the West, only a few women (7.4 percent) came from that region. Then, as today, students preferred to enroll in programs near their homes and families. Thus, states that had library schools—for example, Illinois and New York—produced larger numbers of graduate librarians.

Although historians have defined the term "progressive" in a variety of ways, Robert N. Crunden offers a useful interpretation that categorizes the first generation of progressives as women and men born during the twenty-year period beginning in 1854, and the second generation as those born in a twenty-year period beginning in 1875. According to this definition, virtually all of the women in this study can

2.1. *University of Illinois Library School Class of 1900.*
Courtesy University of Illinois Archives

be considered products of the Progressive Era. Raised in an environment that emphasized strict Protestant moral values and education, they often sought careers that provided an outlet for the service that would satisfy their "demanding consciences." One affluent businessman, for example, described his daughter, an applicant for admission to library school in 1896, as "not content to sit down in idleness or to spend her time entirely in the dissipations of society." Indeed, many Progressive-Era women and men looked to the newly established professions of social work, journalism, and librarianship as outlets for their reforming zeal.[1]

Such socioeconomic indicators as religious affiliation and father's occupation are difficult to establish, yet available data suggest that western librarians, for the most part, came from middle- and upper-middle-class families. A sampling of fathers' occupations includes such white-collar work as diplomat, minister, educator, physician, merchant, and manufacturer. Although census records identify some fathers as farmers and stone masons, they do not indicate whether the men

Table 2.1 Background of Women Librarians Who Worked in the West, 1900–17, N=311

	Year of Library School Graduation:				
	To 1900 N=23	1901–5 N=47	1906–10 N=68	1911–15 N=110	1916–17 N=63
Birthplace:					
Northeastern United States (12.6%)	3	9	8	14	5
Southeastern United States (1.9%)	0	2	0	2	2
Central United States (42.1%)	9	25	37	42	18
Western United States (7.4%)	0	3	6	9	5
Other* (1.6%)	1	1	0	1	2
Unknown (34.4%)	10	7	17	42	31
Marital Status: Formerly Married** (2.6%)	0	1	3	3	1
Married After Library School (23.2%)	3	7	13	30	19
Teaching Experience Before Library School*** (10.3%)	4	2	12	11	3

*Other includes one each from Canada, China, and Sweden, and two from Germany.

**All are widows except for one divorcee (1916–17).

***Data for work prior to library school are incomplete and this figure may underrepresent previous teaching experience.

Source: Author's database.

owned land and quarries or if they were blue-collar workers. Nearly three fourths of the western librarians for whom religious affiliation is known were Presbyterian, Congregational, or Episcopalian, faiths that stressed education and service (see Table 2.2). An additional 9 percent of these women identified themselves as Methodist, but such religions as Unitarian, Christian Science, Society of Friends, Baptist, Catholic, Disciples, and Lutheran had only nominal representation.

Table 2.2 Religious Affiliation of Women Librarians
Who Worked in the West, 1900–17, N=311

Affiliation	Number
Presbyterian	34
Congregational	29
Episcopalian	22
Methodist	12
Unitarian	6
Christian Science	3
Society of Friends	3
Christian	2
Baptist	1
Catholic	1
Disciples	1
Lutheran	1
Unknown	196

Note: Of the 37 percent of the women for whom religious affiliation is known, 74 percent were Presbyterian, Congregational, or Episcopalian.
Source: Author's database.

Although many of these women enjoyed the social, cultural, and educational advantages that accompanied their middle-class status, evidence suggests that some of their families lost ground financially during the late nineteenth and early twentieth centuries. As college students, it had been necessary for a number of librarians to obtain such part-time work as housekeeping and typing to earn money for tuition, books, and lodging. When Charlotte A. Baker enrolled in the Denver Public Library Training Class in 1895, she described many of her classmates as single women who lived at home and wished to earn a little "pin money."[2]

Daughters of working-class families encountered some obstacles when they applied to library schools, most of which emphasized the importance of a student's cultural and educational background. The few working-class women who gained admission to early library schools encountered even greater difficulties securing employment after graduation. Employers preferred to appoint women who possessed backgrounds similar to the library's predominantly white-collar clientele. Thus letters of reference for women who sought admission to library schools stressed their cultural credentials, mentioning that they had "always lived in an intellectual atmosphere and enjoyed social advantages," that they were used to receiving cultured people, or that they had spent time abroad and had been exposed to "the best things in life and literature."[3]

As a result, most early library school students shared a common literary heritage and subscribed to the same cultural, intellectual, and literary canons. Although little is known about how the library school women decoded the books they read, it appears that reading represented more than a passive form of cultural consumption. A profusion of self-study, reading, and literary clubs encouraged late-nineteenth-century women to immerse themselves in the printed word. The very act of reading, at a time when the influence of the printed word was at a peak, fostered "new self-definitions" and "innovative behavior" in many Progressive-era women.[4] Thus, some of the era's literature empowered female readers by presenting models of women who succeeded outside of the family context and in the larger public sphere.

Applications for admission to library school typically contained questions about the nature and extent of students' reading. Although it is likely that some applicants structured their answers to gain approval and admission, their responses provide some indication of the influence of books on their lives. Many described themselves as voracious readers—"I have read everything that has fallen under my hand," or "Since a child of eight I have read constantly." The nature of their reading, however, ranged from highly structured to informal and haphazard. Those who claimed to have read with a purpose indicated that they favored history, drama, psychology, and sociology, and that some of their favorite authors included Charles Dickens, Nathaniel Hawthorne, Francis Parkman, and John Ruskin. One teacher emphasized that she tried to read "as much as possible along the lines of my work," but she also mentioned reading "as widely as possible in all fields of new books, meanwhile trying to extend my knowledge of the older ones." A few women, however, admitted that they had not followed "any special line of reading," or that they had read "a great deal of fiction, some very poor, but most of it the best." Especially popular at the turn of the century were such best-selling titles as Owen Wister's *The Virginian*, Kate Douglas Wiggin's *Rebecca of Sunnybrook Farm*, and *The Masquerader* by Katherine Cecil Thurston.[5]

Mary E. Hazeltine, in an effort to ensure that her Wisconsin Library School students shared a literary heritage, required each woman to become "intimately acquainted" with certain books prior to their arrival in the fall.[6] The list, which varied only slightly between 1907 and 1921, included such standard works of fiction as *Pride and Prejudice, Innocents Abroad, David Copperfield, Ivanhoe,* and *Vanity Fair;* essays by Ralph Waldo Emerson, Charles Lamb, and J. R. Lowell; plays by John Galsworthy and Henrik Ibsen; anthologies of British and American poetry; such works of travel, history, and sociology as Francis Parkman's *Montcalm and Wolfe,* Lafcadio Hearn's *Japan, an Attempt at Interpretation;* and Jane Addams's *Democracy and Social Ethics.* Hazeltine, who believed that the library school curriculum should revolve around the book, expected students to read and digest these works before their first recitation in her course in book selection. At a time when the public increasingly demanded recreational reading, Hazeltine continued to prepare graduates who, through their familiarity with "good" books, would be capable of guiding readers. Employers, like library school directors, believed that good reading promoted good social behavior. As a result, they sometimes required librarians to read and report on books at monthly staff meetings.

The first generation of library school women lived at a time of increasing educational opportunities for women. Most graduated from high schools, many of them coeducational, and a number of the cultural crusaders attended normal schools, colleges, and universities before they decided to become librarians. Nearly three fourths of the women who became western librarians spent one or more years as a normal school, college, or university student, and 60.8 percent earned a bachelor's degree (see Table 2.3). Another 4.5 percent earned college degrees after they became librarians, and at least 6.1 percent eventually earned master's degrees.

The majority of these women matriculated at state universities, but a number graduated from such prestigious women's colleges as Smith, Vassar, and Wellesley and from such private coeducational schools as the University of Chicago and Stanford University (see Table 2.4). Their studies, which ranged from music to education to engineering to typewriting and stenography, reflect both a desire to satisfy intellectual interests and a recognition that women needed some pragmatic skills in the work place. Contemporary observers commented on their seemingly insatiable appetites for knowledge and profound commitment to the pursuit of education. The director of the Riverside School of Li-

Table 2.3 Education Attained by Women Librarians Who Worked in the West, 1900–17, N=311

	Year of Library School Graduation:				
To 1900 N=23	1901–5 N=47	1906–10 N=68	1911–15 N=110	1916–17 N=63

No B. A. degree or unknown (22%)

| 10 | 10 | 15 | 22 | 12 |

Attended college but did not graduate (12.5%)

| 3 | 12 | 9 | 9 | 6 |

Earned B.A. degree before library school (60.8%)

| 8 | 24 | 42 | 75 | 40 |

Years elapsed between B.A. degree and library school graduation:

| 7.0 | 4.2 | 6.2 | 4.2 | 3.46 |

Earned B.A. degree after library school (4.5%)

| 2 | 1 | 2 | 4 | 5 |

Earned M.A. degree after library school (6.1%)

| 1 | 3 | 5 | 8 | 2 |

Attended a second library school (4.5%)

| 0 | 1 | 3 | 8 | 2 |

Source: Author's database.

brary Service described twins enrolled in his school as possessing an "education mania." It was "not merely a whim or desire," he concluded, "but a serious purpose with both of them."[7]

Although Melvil Dewey promoted librarianship as a suitable occupation for the college-educated woman, a bachelor's degree was not required for admission to library schools before 1902, when the New York State Library School instituted that requirement. Until that time, schools required as little as a high school diploma or its equivalent, and an entrance examination for admission. As a result, library education became accessible to older, or nontraditional students. Women beyond the traditional age for admission to college, women whose families could not afford higher education, and women who left college before graduation, regarded the one- or two-year library school course as a pragmatic educational alternative that would allow them to enter a professional line of work after a relatively brief period of study.

Approximately 12.5 percent of these women withdrew from college before completing their undergraduate education. In most cases they cited a lack of funds or a desire to obtain work so they would be

Table 2.4 Selected List of Colleges and Universities
Attended by Women Librarians Who Worked in the West,
1900–17, in Order of Frequency

Earned B.A. degree from:	Number
University of Washington	33
Stanford University	12
University of Illinois	10
Smith College	10
University of Nebraska	8
University of Minnesota	7
University of Wisconsin	7
Wellesley College	7
Pomona College	6
University of California	6
University of Chicago	6
University of Michigan	6
University of Oregon	6
University of Iowa	5
Iowa State University	5
Carleton College	4
Simmons College	4
University of Colorado	4
Vassar College	4
Western Reserve University	4

Source: Author's database.

able to assist younger siblings who also wished to acquire a college education. Others withdrew to return home as caretakers for ailing or elderly relatives, and later found it difficult to resume their studies. Women who lacked college degrees sometimes expressed feelings of inadequacy. One, who described her earlier education as sadly neglected, regretted that she could not "face the ordeal [speaking in public] with the equanimity the modern girl has been trained to do."[8]

As time passed and professional standards emerged, the lack of a bachelor's degree became more and more of a disadvantage for library school graduates. When the preceptress of the Wisconsin Library School recommended a high school graduate for a position in 1913, she observed that "her greatest weakness is, perhaps, on the knowledge of books, due to less education . . . it is a lack that she will never be able to fully overcome."[9] Again, library leaders shared a belief in the ideology of reading, and expected their students to share a common literary canon.

Library schools that educated the largest numbers of western librarians included the New York State Library School, the University of Illinois, Pratt Institute, and the University of Wisconsin (see Table 2.5). College graduates tended to gravitate to the New York State Library School and the University of Illinois Library School, both known for their high admission requirements. While these two programs offered a two-year curriculum, it was possible to obtain work after finishing the junior year. Most library schools of this period, however, required only one year of study.

Women who left library schools after their junior year sometimes enrolled in other library school programs for a second year of more specialized study. One institution that offered such work was the Training School for Children's Librarians in Pittsburgh. More women pursued this course during the second decade of the twentieth century, as children's library work expanded. As Table 2.3 illustrates, at least 4.5 percent of the western librarians earned a second library school certificate.

The typical library school student of this era was in her late twenties, although the women in this study ranged in age from nineteen to fifty-six when they graduated from library school.[10] Given their older average age, women librarians may have been less likely to consider librarianship a temporary interlude than younger women entering the work force. Directors of library schools generally preferred to limit admission to applicants between the ages of eighteen and thirty, believing as they did that younger women were not yet ready to leave home and that older, less-flexible students would "take to new conditions with difficulty" and would have trouble securing employment.[11] Nonetheless, exceptions occurred, as in the case of a widowed Ida A. Kidder who entered the University of Illinois Library School at the age of fifty. Known affectionately by her classmates as "Mother Kidder," she had an active career in western libraries despite her age and crippling rheumatism.

The women who graduated from library school prior to 1901 generally allowed seven years to elapse between the receipt of their bachelor's degrees and library school certificates. During this time some lived at home and cared for relatives while others taught school. Data for employment prior to library school are incomplete, but at least 10

Table 2.5 Women Librarians Who Worked in the West, 1900–17, By Year of Their First Western Position, Type of Position, State, and Library School Attended, N=279*

	Date of First Western Position:				
	To 1900	1901–5	1906–10	1911–15	1916–17
Number of women appointed:	4	30	63	120	62
Average age at first western position:	25.3	29.7	33.2	29.0	29.7
First position in: Academic library (25.8%)	2	13	19	24	14
Public library (62.0%)	2	9	37	86	39
School libraries (5.0%)	—	2	1	5	6
Special libraries (2.9%)	—	2	2	3	1
State libraries (3.2%)	—	3	4	2	0
Library school (1.1%)	—	1	—	—	2
Location of First Position: Arizona (.7%)	1	—	—	—	1
California (27.2%)	1	12	11	32	20
Colorado (5.01%)	—	2	3	7	2
Idaho (1.8%)	—	2	2	1	0
Montana (4.7%)	1	3	4	2	3
Nevada (.4%)	—	—	—	1	—
New Mexico (1.4%)	—	2	1	1	—
Oregon (15.4%)	—	4	15	18	6
Utah (.7%)	1	—	—	—	1

(*continued*)

Table 2.5 Women Librarians Who Worked in the West, 1900–17, By Year of Their First Western Position, Type of Position, State, and Library School Attended, N=279* (*continued*)

	Date of First Western Position:				
To 1900	1901–5	1906–10	1911–15	1916–17
Washington (40.9%)					
—	5	27	55	27
Wyoming (1.8%)					
—	—	—	3	2
Library Schools Attended: New York State (23.7%)					
3	11	19	25	8
Pratt Institute (8.9%)					
1	5	3	14	2
Drexel Institute (.7%)					
—	1	1	—	—
University of Illinois (23.7%)					
—	13	23	21	9
Pittsburgh (4.3%)					
—	—	3	6	3
Simmons College (3.9%)					
—	—	6	4	1
Western Reserve University (1.8%)					
—	—	—	4	1
Indiana Library School (.7%)					
—	—	1	—	1
Wisconsin Library School (8.2%)					
—	—	7	12	4
New York Public Library (3.6%)					
—	—	—	4	6
University of Washington (14.3%)					
—	—	—	22	18
Riverside School of Library Service (.7%)					
—	—	—	—	2
Los Angeles Public Library (5.4%)					
—	—	—	8	7

Source: Author's database.

*32 cases have been excluded because they are incomplete.

percent taught in public schools (see Table 2.1). Discouraged by low salaries and by the lack of cultural opportunities in the rural communities where they taught, some regarded their years of teaching as drudgery. They became anxious to make a change and looked to librarianship as an occupation well-suited to their backgrounds. Many teachers thought that library work would be less taxing physically. One concluded, after spending several years as an instructor in a girls' seminary, that a woman "can spend too many years [in a school setting] . . . such a life is not a desirable one." Another commented that her time as a teacher had consisted of "many years of worry and physical work beyond my strength."[12] Teachers also entered library work because they regarded it as another form of educational service. Their years in the classroom had shown them how vital it was to improve students' access to books and periodicals.

Others had worked as assistants in their local public libraries while they were in high school, and as college students a number of women worked on a part-time basis as student librarians. One woman recalled that her brief experience as a student assistant had "convinced me that I can do the work, and enjoy it." Also, college librarians sometimes encouraged promising students to consider a library career. And the untrained women who worked as amateur librarians began to enroll in library schools when they recognized that professional training was the key to increasing their salaries, ensuring their reappointments, and improving their prospects for advancement.[13]

Librarianship also appealed to other groups of working women who sought more challenging and rewarding employment. One, restless and frustrated with her prospects for advancement, declared: "The thought of selling grape juice at the Emporium, or perhaps a suit to Mr. Daniels the next [time] he is in town does not appeal and I really think I am better fitted for other things." Another, a postal clerk, described herself as a prisoner sitting behind the bars of the general delivery window "handing out stamps and money orders and smiling at the dear P.O. public."[14] Other women delayed their professional development until the death of a parent or spouse made it possible, even necessary, to choose a life work.

Only a few had worked in male-dominated fields before entering library school. Grace Raymond Hebard, the first woman to major in engineering at the University of Iowa, recalled that she "met with many discouragements and many sneers, and much opposition to my enrolling in the scientific course, which was then entirely a man's college." A staunch suffragist, she accepted a position with the U.S. Surveyor General's Office in Cheyenne, Wyoming Territory, in 1882. In 1889 she spoke on behalf of women's suffrage before the Wyoming State Constitutional Convention. A personal friend of Carrie Chapman Catt, Hebard traveled throughout the country speaking on behalf of universal suffrage. When satisfactory opportunities for a female engineer began to elude her, Hebard moved to Laramie and became secretary and member of the board of trustees, professor of political economy, and librarian at the University of Wyoming. Although she lacked formal library training, Hebard served as librarian from 1894 until 1919, albeit without compensation, and became the first president of the state library association. One of a small number of women faculty at the University of Wyoming, Hebard made her home, first with Irene May Morse and then with Agnes Mathilde Wergeland, both professors of history. Wergeland shared Hebard's love of the out-of-doors and sports.[15] Another western librarian entered the profession nearly twenty years after earning a medical degree from Northwestern University and serving as a medical missionary in Africa.[16]

These women, however, are exceptions. Librarians typically are not viewed as suffragettes or feminists, and there is little evidence in the cultural crusaders' surviving correspondence to challenge this assumption. Most appear to have taken a moderate course. When Ida Kidder proposed in 1919 that Oregon State Librarian Cornelia Marvin be sent to Congress, she declared:

> I have never been a suffragist, but if suffrage must come, I want the education and development of women to go on to the point where they would really perform these duties efficiently.[17]

Kidder, who found it distasteful when she had to give "sex talks" to the college women, did not share Marvin's zeal for suffrage. She cautioned her friend: "I fear you are exercising a great influence in favor of suffrage by your close touch with legislators and other public officials."[18] Such fears, however, did not discourage Marvin, who also used her position to circulate Socialist literature to her colleagues and to campaign actively for the abolishment of capital punishment.

Librarians who moved west from states that had not yet granted women suffrage regarded their right to vote with curiosity, if not with enthusiasm. Several mailed pamphlets about their newly acquired rights to friends and family in the eastern United States. A Montana librarian found Jeannette Rankin's 1917 campaign "very thrilling" even though she took very little part in it. She hoped that the women of the Wisconsin Library school soon would have suffrage so they too could partake in the "interesting" experience of voting:

> When you stand before a ballot you find you don't think the
> things you thought you thought at all. You have your mind
> all crammed with principles, and yet you find yourself voting
> for John Brown because he has six children and only one
> leg after all.[19]

Although library work appears to have had less appeal for suffragettes, the women who chose to take it up were anything but stereotypical. Letters of reference described some as social favorites, attractive, public-spirited, charming, independent, and poised, while referring to others as "lacking in self-reliance," "utterly lacking in boisterousness or self-assertiveness, perhaps almost too shy for successful service."[20] Library school directors hastened to assure prospective employers that women who were petite in stature nonetheless possessed personalities that would inspire confidence from the very beginning.

In communities where the library was a new undertaking, library boards placed a great deal of emphasis on the librarian's appearance and social skills because they expected her to promote the cause. Western employers, unable to conduct personal interviews with applicants for most positions, often required them to submit photographs, which they believed would provide clues about a librarian's health, age, and personality. In a number of instances, employers based their hiring decisions on "the personal qualities which seemed to be indicated by the photograph."[21]

Extreme youth, along with inexperience, represented a different type of disadvantage for women who wished to work in the West. Although employers believed that youthful candidates possessed enthusiasm, eagerness, energy, and good intentions, they expressed concern about peculiarities that they attributed almost entirely to youth. Such traits included being "too impulsive" or having "too many irons in the fire to do everything" well.[22] Employers also feared that young women would find it difficult to live apart from their mothers, especially for the first time.

Although the stereotype of the librarian is often that of a spinster, approximately one fourth of the women in this study married after working as librarians (see Table 2.1), and a small number entered the profession after being widowed or divorced. This marriage rate is slightly higher than the findings of a 1921 Carnegie Corporation report, which reported that nearly 22 percent of all women who graduated from library school between 1887 and 1921 married.[23] As the data in Table 2.1 indicate, women graduates after 1910 allowed fewer years to elapse between college and library school graduation, and a higher percentage married.

At the turn of the century women married at an average age of twenty-two. Those who became librarians typically entered the profession during their late twenties and early thirties, and many probably did not expect to marry. Some women felt that interest in marriage would suggest a lack of commitment to the profession. Upon learning of another librarian's marriage, one woman emphatically declared:

> Please do not imagine that I am going to follow in [her] footsteps . . . because I am not. There have not yet been inducements strong enough for that, and at my advanced years, I fear there will never be.

Others jokingly referred to themselves as "spinster-at-large" and boasted of being in "no danger" of being married off. Hebard's photograph album, documenting her life with Irene May Morse, bore the title "Old Maid's Paradise," and one photo caption proclaimed:

> *They say they prefer to marital strife*
> *Their own independent and feminine life:*
> *Truthful old maids!*[24]

A few even expressed puzzlement when they learned of colleagues who had married. One "couldn't understand why any one who had reached such a height in [her career] . . . would descend to be married."[25]

Nevertheless, library school directors—especially male directors—often expected that younger students would be "safely married off."

Employers frequently shared this view. Indeed, Charlotte Baker took vicarious pleasure in planning the weddings of her Colorado State Agricultural College assistants:

> Then I married off Miss Walker on Wednesday . . . Her
> father was too old to help her, and her mother was away . . .
> I planned the decorations and helped place them. I
> planned the refreshments . . . and lastly I engaged the
> preacher. Can you imagine me as Best Man?

That Baker associated marriage with security and comfort is evident. After a colleague at the University of Denver married in 1914, Baker conveyed her congratulations and commented that the woman must be glad that she did not have "to go back to the grind of library work this fall." To another, she wrote: "I am very glad to hear . . . that you are in a home of your own."[26]

Youthful librarians sent letters to library school directors announcing when their hearts had been "stolen quite away" or they had "foresaken [*sic*] the realms of spinsterhood." A graduate of the Riverside School of Library Service, who married two years after completing that program, assured the director that although she had enjoyed library work, having a home of her own "beats even that."[27]

Some of the western librarians rejoiced at the prospect of quitting work after they married, but others confessed to having "a very queer feeling" about leaving their libraries. One wrote that life "would be only a partial existence without the library atmosphere." Although announcements of engagements and marriages elicited joyful responses from library school directors, they also contained assurances that married women could continue to serve the library cause: "You will still be a leader in all good things in the community to which you are going, so I shall still think of you as a library worker."[28]

Most women resigned from library work upon marriage, but a number of those who married late in life continued working. A husband's ill health made it necessary for several librarians to return to the work force. A married woman who applied for a position in 1904 expressed concern that she might be refused because of her marital status. She gave as her reason for seeking work the fact that her husband had "softening of the brain." Another woman, widowed in her mid-thirties, wanted to work because of financial need, but she also thought that her days in the library would help her forget her loss. Finally, a few women found themselves "at liberty for another position" after something happened to their lovers, and one woman returned to work at the Public Library of Portland after being divorced. Library director Mary Frances Isom assured Cornelia Marvin that "there was absolutely no breath of scandal connected with her divorce" and that the librarian had taken back her maiden name in the hope that the experience could be forgotten.[29]

Forgoing marriage did not necessarily mean a childless existence. On several occasions western women librarians adopted young girls, although little documentation has survived to explain what motivated them. A librarian in the Midwest, upon learning that western colleague had adopted a daughter, exclaimed: "I'm glad you have a little girl—I'm sure she is a pleasure & comfort—mine is!" Oregon's Mary Frances Isom adopted a young girl, as did Belle Sweet and her sister in Idaho. And although Charlotte Baker regretted that she never had children, she rejoiced when a former assistant named her daughter Charlotte: "I have a real live BABY named after me. What do you think of that!"[30]

Like many of the early female college graduates, western librarians struggled to accommodate both the family claim and their own desire for an independent, professional life. Even after women left home for college or career, the family had shaped their expectations and had set limits on their expectations. As Joyce Antler illustrates, the college experience alone, with its "vague and unformulated" social claim, was not powerful enough to break the claim of the patriarchal family.[31] Thus, on one level it appears that families supported their daughters' pursuit of education and their goal of becoming professional women; on another it is obvious that the library school experience reinforced, rather than challenged, traditional societal roles. Instead, the library school experience created and reinforced a shared identity among women who later would be challenged by external forces.

It is doubtful that many of these librarians had an opportunity to establish a sense of self-identity, apart from that of daughter or sister, before they enrolled in library school. Although more than half attended college, they often matriculated at schools near their homes. Moreover, mothers sometimes accompanied their daughters to college and to library school, serving as companions, chaperons, and housekeepers. Library school directors and faculty further reinforced the family claim, adopting a maternalistic stance toward their protégées and helping them to accommodate family demands. They did so by attempting to place women near their families or in positions that accommodated health limitations or that allowed for the greatest degree of personal growth.

Graduate librarians articulated their appreciation and vowed to be worthy of the confidence that had been placed in them. Katharine Sharp's students at the University of Illinois knew that she was interested in their progress and that she wanted to learn about the success of her "old library girls." Letters conveyed their appreciation in such statements as "I should be very ungrateful if I did not try to do all I could for the credit of your department" or that a woman vowed to "do the right thing as a representative of the school."[32]

At first glance, one might expect that work in a distant location—the American West—would reinforce the professional claim and perhaps erode the family claim. Closer inspection, however, suggests that this was not always the case. Western women librarians fell into three categories: the mature woman accompanied by her mother or another relative, often female; the young woman who ventured into the work place, but returned home frequently, sometimes abandoning her career; and the woman who enjoyed a significant degree of autonomy. The first two categories appear to have predominated.

A number of the western women began careers as librarians while at the same time caring for a widowed parent. These women sometimes lived relatively autonomous lives until their youngest sibling left home, but they seldom challenged the idea that their mothers ultimately would live with them. A newly appointed librarian at the University of California, in Berkeley, reported that "Miss Carroll has rented a small house, furnished, and expects her mother soon to keep house with her. Miss Burt, the new accession clerk from Pratt [Institute Library School], has her mother with her too."[33] Evidence indicates that a number of employers believed that women who were accompanied by their mothers would be more stable employees and that they would be less likely to change positions.

In such instances, librarians made career decisions based on what would be best for the parent. They gave as reasons for seeking western employment the fact that the West's "more equable climate" would suit an ailing mother, or that a complete change of scenery would ease a widowed father's grief.[34] Because a father's work typically took priority over a daughter's career, librarians often expressed the hope that they would be able to accept work in other locations after their fathers had retired.

This strong sense of daughterly devotion made it difficult for women to plan their careers. One agonized because she could not afford to be without a position, yet felt she was needed at home: "I want to do the right thing and I am so undecided as to what the right thing is." Others were troubled when their fathers, not recognizing that most library salaries were low, discouraged them from accepting positions that did not appear to be financially rewarding. Those who were eager to become independent, at least economically, sometimes ignored fatherly advice and accepted low-paid positions. In such cases, they justified their actions by explaining that their families were "too prejudiced" or that parents had exaggerated their abilities. Thus, through self-deprecation they could gain a measure of independence.[35]

A consequence of being accompanied by one's mother, especially one who had health problems, was that the daughter became less geographically mobile. In a number of instances, librarians accepted or declined positions based on their mothers' preferences. One librarian, debating whether or not to apply for a position, observed: "I scarcely know what to say about the position in Oregon as my mother is not anxious to go so far west." When discussing a colleague who also worked as a librarian in Portland, one librarian observed that her friend wanted to make a change, but questioned "whether her mother would let her leave town." And when considering two positions, both which paid less than she earned at the University of Wyoming, one librarian opted for a post at Washington State College because "it is near enough my family that I hope to be able to have my mother with me."[36]

It was not uncommon for families to summon their librarian daughters home to attend to an ill family member or to become a companion to a elderly relative. Several women gave up western positions after parents insisted that they return home for extended vacations or to nurse ill relatives. After the death of her sister, one librarian's parents became "especially dependent on her" and, although she wanted to work in the West, she believed that it was her duty to relocate near them so she could go home every weekend. Others resigned positions because their parents wanted them to rest. A librarian at the Los Angeles Public Library fully expected to return there after her vacation, but instead submitted her resignation because "my family thought it best."[37]

The ease with which parents called their daughters home implies that they lacked commitment to their daughters' careers. It also suggests that some of these women assumed that they could stop and start positions with relative ease. During the profession's formative years, library school directors took this in stride, encouraging women to fulfill their family obligations and stressing their willingness to find places for the women when they were free to resume work. As the years passed, even library school directors began to admonish women who changed positions too frequently, or those who complained that their salaries and vacations did not permit them to visit families in the East or Midwest. According to Frances Simpson, a faculty member at the University of Illinois Library School, this was one of the "things which hampers women in the profession." She continued:

> It is not the public's business to know or to care whether its librarian's family lives in Spokane or Chicago. They are not paying for traveling expenses. When a man takes a position of that sort, to a certain extent he cuts loose from his family, and he expects to make his home where his work is. Women seem to find a great deal of difficulty in making up their minds to do that.[38]

Given the number of women who resigned positions to assist with home responsibilities, it is not surprising that some employers began to doubt that these women were committed to library work. They sometimes vented frustrations with women who quit, seemingly without warning. After a number of such experiences, one library director exclaimed:

> I want someone who is willing to come West and *stay* West, and who will not feel at liberty to give up the department position at any time because of the desire to be nearer her family or be called East because of illness in the family.[39]

Finally, a third group of women achieved autonomous lives, although they sometimes delayed their entrance into the profession until the death of a parent. Such was the case of Mary Frances Isom, who cared for her widowed father until his death. Only then, at the age of thirty-six, did she enroll in library school and accept her first western position. Likewise, Lena Brownell viewed her "whole future" as an "untried field" after the death of her mother.[40]

These, then, were the women who read the popular and professional literature that abounded with accounts of opportunities for employment and innovation in western life and work. The examples of several women who had given up secure positions in eastern and midwestern libraries in exchange for pioneering work in California, Oregon, or New Mexico inspired many:

> I think of the opportunities of the West and the library
> activity which is already established in Oregon, then too that
> both you and Miss Kennedy considered it worth giving up
> Wisconsin positions for Oregon . . . I find I cannot quite get
> away from considering it.[41]

While an ambitious woman could expect to find more employment opportunities in industrialized eastern cities than in the rural West, a number of early graduate librarians expressed eagerness for western work. Those who had entered the profession motivated by a desire to serve society regarded the West, at the beginning stages of cultural development, as a tabula rasa. Even as late as 1917 a University of Illinois graduate expressed her conviction that "the library movement is so new in the West that it seemed to me if I could get a foothold there, there would be a good opportunity to grow up with the libraries."[42] While recent graduates believed that the West held the promise of excellent professional experience, women employed as subordinates in eastern and midwestern libraries regarded it as a place where they could develop executive ability.

Librarians also believed, somewhat mistakenly, that western salaries would be larger than those paid in eastern and midwestern libraries. These ideas were in part fostered by articles claiming that "remuneration increases steadily as one goes farther west." In letters of application women routinely mentioned dissatisfaction with their salaries and prospects for advancement. An Elkhart, Indiana, librarian exclaimed in 1909:

I am tired of working for the low salary paid in this part of the country, and feel that with my experience and knowledge . . . I ought to be in a position where my opportunities would be greater.[43]

Even when salaries were comparable to those they already earned, women believed that they could save more in the West because they expected the cost of living to be lower.

Others sought western work because they admired the region. Brief encounters, while on vacation or during temporary assignments, triggered in many the desire to live there permanently: "I have experienced 'the call of the wild' too insistently to mistake its meaning," wrote one. Another claimed that she would "be willing to make sacrifices in salary because the locality and spirit of the [western] people" would be "sufficient recompense." A third woman acknowledged that while her desire to live in the West might be a passing fancy, "taking a position there is the only thing that will ever get it out of my system."[44]

The West's reputation for a hospitable climate also appealed to women plagued by ill health, especially respiratory ailments. They believed that drier climates, such as California and Colorado, would restore them. Katharine Sharp, for example, sought positions in warm climates for graduates troubled with asthma. Women also moved West in the hope that the climate would improve the health of their children or elderly parents.

When library school directors nominated students for western library positions, they often commented on the women's ability to adapt to new climates and communities. The preceptress of the Wisconsin Library School emphasized that her candidate for a position in Montana was "fully acclimated to the climate of both North Dakota and Montana" and furthermore would understand "the conditions of life in the communities of our newer Western states."[45] Employers found such women desirable not only because they believed them to be less likely to become homesick, but also because it would be easier for them to acclimate to western life and become leaders within the community.

Many wanted to join parents, brothers, and sisters who recently had migrated West: "My people are moving to Idaho and . . . I feel it is my duty to go too." A Deer Lodge, Montana, woman, devoted to her home and family, would not even consider an eastern position because of her great desire to be within reasonable distance of her home. While other natives of the West found eastern salaries and positions tempting, they often declined because "the places are so far away," explaining that their parents wanted them to live near home. As a result, they sometimes ignored the advice of library school directors and accepted semiprofessional work—becoming stenographers or poorly paid library assistants instead of directors—in order to obtain western employment.[46]

Women whose parents and siblings moved to such cities as Los Angeles, Portland, or Seattle, had greater opportunities for library work than did those who joined families in rural communities. One graduate, after filing applications with nearly every Colorado library in 1900, concluded that if a position did not become available soon "I will have to turn my attention to some other line of work for which I am not prepared." Families sometimes attempted to exert influence on well-placed friends in order to secure positions for their daughters. Margaret Sweet, for example, appealed to an Idaho judge to give her sister, a recent graduate of the University of Illinois Library School, the position of librarian in a recently constructed Carnegie library. Much to her disappointment, the librarian already had been elected.[47]

The professional librarians in this study worked in every western state, with California, Oregon, and Washington employing the majority (see Table 2.5). Library development lagged in several states during this era, as is evident by the employment of only one librarian in Nevada, three in Arizona, and five each in New Mexico and Wyoming. The presence of several nationally visible library workers in California and Oregon undoubtedly contributed to the larger numbers of professional librarians who began their careers in those two states, while the creation of a library school at the University of Washington made it possible for that state to begin producing and employing larger numbers of professionally trained librarians. Thus, it was in the nation's library schools that many of the women in this study acquired the library spirit, and it was in the American West that they chose to put it to work.

~ three ~

Initial Impressions

The librarians who journeyed West during the early twentieth century often traveled on special days when immigrants' and land seekers' tickets became available at reduced prices. Sometimes they took advantage of stops in Chicago or other cities along the way, visiting libraries and gathering supplies that would be unavailable in smaller western communities. University of Idaho librarian Belle Sweet, who traveled by train from Iowa to Idaho in 1905, recalled sitting on a wooden bench in a car that had "a great big pot belly stove in the end" for cooking and heating. Many found the journey long and tiresome, and they required several days to recover before beginning work. Arduous journeys, however, did not dampen their enthusiasm for "such wonderful things in nature . . . as any of us would go round the world to see or spend any amount of time or money we could afford."[1]

Their initial letters to friends and families exclaimed about the towering snow-capped mountains, and contained frequent references to such places as the newly established Glacier National Park and Pike's Peak. A librarian in Portland wished that all of her teachers and classmates could be with her, "enjoying the beautiful spring weather . . . the crocuses and daffodils . . . and the birds singing so that I can hardly believe it is only the middle of March." Others praised the mild climate and fruit trees and flowers blooming in profusion there—"it is like walking through fairyland"—while a woman who took up residence further inland spoke fondly of the gentle Polouse, flowing through southeastern Washington, and of the combined harvesters drawn by thirty-two horses in the wheat fields surrounding Pullman.[2]

Awed by the West's geographic beauty, they nonetheless expressed concern about conservation issues and the exploitation of the land by eastern investors. Many provided library school directors with candid descriptions of frontier communities with their vacant lots, numerous construction projects, and unpaved streets. When Charlotte Baker, a native of New York, arrived in Las Cruces, New Mexico, in 1900, she observed a town that

> had but two buildings that were two stories high, the rest of the town being adobe structures. The tiny college settlement had some brick college buildings surrounded by a few adobe dwellings. We had no sewage, no lights, no pavements. We dug wells for water and had a landscape dotted with windmills. For fuel, we burned wood that was hauled in from the mountains.

Her successor, who arrived six years later, thought that she "had been dropped into Jericho . . . the houses, low and rambling, with very few windows and those very small." She expressed relief, however, after discovering that a few of the adobe homes featured such touches of civilization as Chippendale chairs and mahogany furniture.[3]

The newly appointed public librarian in Hoquiam, Washington, proclaimed it to be one of the "most unattractive cities" she had ever seen. Built on tide lands with many dikes and "almost a total absence of green grass or trees," it looked even worse during a rainy season. The presence of industry (that is, sawmills and factories) dominated other communities. Inadequate supplies of water hampered development in a number of communities. Although the official catalog of the State Normal School described Cheney, Washington, as "one of the most delightful towns of Eastern Washington . . . supplied with an abundance of pure spring water," a librarian who lived there several years later concluded that the main reason for its "standstill is its lack of water power—there is no river or lake of sufficient size near here." Others found the lack of railroads to be a "serious handicap" to library, as well as community, development.[4]

Nearby, Roxana Johnson found Pullman, Washington, to be "a rather impossible place to live," one to which she would either have to become "deadened or reconsiled [sic]." In addition to the lack of cultural stimulation, Johnson deplored the town's hills: "How even through political pulls they ever located a state school on these hills is beyond me." She was especially frustrated after attempting to do her weekly marketing:

> I went down in town (a mile down hill all the way—and as a
> most natural consequence—up hill all the way back). . . .
> After leaving my orders at the various stores I winded my
> way to a meat market. I ordered enough meat of various
> kinds to last a few days and gave them my address and said
> "Please send it there." He (the clerk) looked at me
> peculiarly and said, "We have no delivery" . . . As a result I
> carried my several days supply up the hill home and . . .
> decided to turn vegetarian.[5]

Most librarians considered local transportation quite primitive, consisting as it usually did of one or two horse-drawn cabs. Belle Sweet recalled that she and other residents of early-twentieth-century Moscow, Idaho, had to depend on "our own two feet or horse-drawn vehicles." During one winter, that community's cab remained frozen in the mud until the ground thawed, while in neighboring Pullman, Washington, the cabman refused to venture out in inclement weather. Good sidewalks also were rare and consisted, in many towns, of loose planks. One librarian was convinced that men had laid the planks just far enough apart to catch the heel of her shoe. Another recalled that "You stepped on the end and the other end would fly up."[6] These and other minor inconveniences, however, served as constant reminders that the librarians had indeed taken up residence in pioneer communities.

A few women experienced difficulty adapting to the higher altitudes. A librarian in Pendleton, Oregon, complained that her head did not "work just right," and others objected to the climate because it was too dry or too moist. Although librarians in New Mexico praised the grays and browns of the desert, they eventually found the excessively dry heat "very wearing year after year."[7]

Dust also made a significant impression because it seemed to be everywhere, coating them, their living quarters, and their books. Sweet recalled attending a livestock show carrying a white linen parasol, only to return home with it "as black as any man's coat and it was ready for the bathtub." Others commented on sand and wind storms. One expressed surprise because the "wind blew with such a force that I positively could not move and . . . it would blow my skirt clear over my head."[8] Although dust storms could be quite exasperating, some librarians looked on the bright side, and came to appreciate the purity and invigorating quality of the atmosphere after such storms.

Dust pervaded the libraries as well as the out-of-doors. Estelle Lutrell, who moved from Chicago to Tucson, Arizona, in 1904, recalled her first glimpse of the University Library:

> Some seven thousand volumes, shelved on cumbersome
> wooden stacks, a few tables covered with oil cloth. . . .
> Newspapers from some of the larger towns in the Territory,
> which had been accumulating throughout the summer . . .
> scattered hither and yon . . . covered with a generous
> coating of Arizona dust.

Evidently her dismay showed, because administrators quickly assured her that Arizona dust was not "the grimy sort common to Chicago."[9] In neighboring New Mexico, Lucy Lewis found it difficult to combat the dust typical of an arid climate:

> Find the dustiest place in your stacks, where books are
> seldom used, and multiply by ten—and you will have an
> idea of the conditions here—where we have only a few
> inches of rainfall during the year.[10]

Snow appears to have made less of an impression on these women, but a librarian in Bozeman, Montana, did find the icy cold and layers of snow that accumulated every few days quite disagreeable. After an unusually severe snow storm hit Moscow, Idaho, Belle Sweet recalled walking down the street in a path made by a horse-drawn snowplow consisting of two painted boards.[11]

Unlike schoolteachers, who often boarded with their pupils' families or members of the school board, librarians had to lodge in hotels, boarding houses, private homes, dormitories and, to a lesser extent, apartments. Although hotels were an option, residence there tended to be temporary because they were more costly. The quality of hotels ranged from a "new place, with very rightly furnished furniture and very greeny green carpets" in Monterey, California, to the Bardin House in Salinas, an establishment which "was dirty beyond words.

The table was fair, but I found absolutely nothing first class but the rates."[12]

Few women expressed concern for their safety when they stayed in hotels, although when Mabel Wilkinson stayed at a Hartville Junction, Wyoming, hotel in 1915, she felt "fortunate . . . to find a front room with a lock on the door." Most of the western librarians appear to have traveled freely and without fear of harm. Wilkinson, who traveled virtually alone for two weeks, did not hesitate to rise in the wee hours of the morning to begin her travels. A California librarian seemed to be puzzled when "someone suggested seeing the sheriff." Although she saw no reason to be alarmed, she did call at the sheriff's office is only to find a deputy, "but he and I got quite friendly, so I guess I'll be well treated if anything happens."[13]

Because few apartment houses existed, most librarians lived in rooming or boarding houses. Of thirty-five assistants employed by the Public Library of Portland in 1910, fully twenty boarded away from their families. Belle Sweet found the residents of Moscow, Idaho, to be "very generous in taking in University people looking for homes," but noted that the warmth of their hospitality could not always compensate for the quality of the room. She remembered her surprise upon learning that one place that the room was "a little cheaper because whoever has it has to keep the fire going to heat the water for the other people living in the place." A Seattle librarian, on the other hand, praised her quarters in the home of a music professor. She enjoyed listening to "fine music" as the professor practiced every evening.[14]

The availability of bathtubs elicited frequent comments, indicating their importance to a number of these western librarians. One, accompanied by her mother, indicated that she could not consider taking a position unless she could be guaranteed adequate bathing facilities. Bathtubs also ranged in quality. Sweet visited one rooming house that boasted a bathroom constructed out of a closet. Inside it housed a crude bathtub made "of tin sheets soldered together and attached by tacks to a wooden frame in the form of a triangle . . . you were supposed to stick your feet in that point, which makes bathing very difficult." Another woman, after bathing, observed that the water fell on the basement floor. She notified her landlady, who was not overly concerned because "nobody ever used a bath-tub very often."[15]

Based on the prices cited by many of the western librarians, room and board consumed at least half of most women's income, ranging from approximately twenty to forty dollars each month at a time when salaries were forty-five to seventy dollars a month. Little remained for clothing, travel, and contributions to siblings and parents. Rooms in Moscow, Idaho, "rented for seven to twenty dollars a month [in 1908] depending on locality and general desirability." In Eugene, Oregon, room and board ranged from four to seven dollars a week that same year, and a librarian could expect to pay from thirty-five to forty dollars a month for housing in Albuquerque, New Mexico, in 1910. Employers boasted that these rates compared favorably with eastern and midwestern communities, but librarians who had been in the West for a time considered them inflated: "The expenses out here," wrote an Idaho librarian in 1909, "are very high. One can secure no good board for less than $5 per week. So you see boarding alone is quite a drain on one's salary."[16]

Sometimes the cost of renting a house compared favorably to a rooming or boarding house, especially if the cost could be shared. In 1913, Cornelia Marvin paid $17.50 per month for a six-room house in Salem, Oregon. She dined out for twenty-five to thirty cents per meal, and considered this a bargain in contrast with "*the best*" board and room which could be had for thirty-five dollars a month. Marvin could afford the luxury of having an entire house to herself, but other librarians found it necessary to let one or more of the rooms to boarders. Librarians in larger communities could live together, but those in rural areas sometimes shared housing with local teachers. Charlotte Baker leased a five-room house in Fort Collins, Colorado, reserving "a sitting room and a bed room for myself," and renting "the rest to a young lady and her brother. She teaches and he goes to school. We all go out to our meals."[17]

Roommates sometimes became substitutes for the family circle, but without the accompanying restraints. A librarian living apart from her family for the first time regarded her arrangements with two high school teachers as a great adventure: "We are having a high time, getting our own meals, stoking our own furnace, and doing as we please." In Los Angeles, nine librarians expressed their delight to be sharing a house, and boasted about their "literary gathering," while three women in Seattle had apartments in the same building and spent their leisure hours together. The newly hired librarian at the *Spokesman Review* rented a room from the director of the Spokane Public Library—"I like her very much, and she has been very kind to me"—but evidently did not dine with her: "It is also only two blocks and a half from the *Spokesman Review,* one block and a half from the Unitarian Church, and the place where I dine is between my room and the office."[18] The two women did, however, spend many hours discussing issues of mutual professional concern.

Two Wisconsin graduates developed such a close friendship that they both sought employment in the same institution. They feared that people would think them "a bit 'queer' in our desire not to go different ways," but they managed to maintain a home together for many years until one finally married, late in life. At the University of Wyoming Grace Raymond Hebard and Professor Agnes Mathilde Wergeland built a home together, "The Doctor's Inn," where they lived until Wergeland's death in 1914.[19]

Women who moved West with their mothers usually preferred to lease several rooms or a house. Because accommodations in many western towns were limited, they sometimes declined appointments or even changed positions when housing did not suit their mothers. Roxana Johnson decided to change positions because her mother found Pullman, Washington, "a rather hard place to live in comfortably."[20]

A number of librarians at normal schools, colleges, and universities had the option of living in dormitories. Prior to her arrival in August 1906, Lucy Lewis was advised that because most Las Cruces, New Mexico, boarding houses would be closed, she would "find it most convenient to room and board at the Girls' Dormitory" along with several other teachers where expenses would be "considerably less" than in town. As a result, Lewis found herself living with eight other "lady teachers" and twenty-eight girls. Ridenbaugh Hall, a women's dormitory, opened at the University of Idaho in 1902, and boasted "comforts, cheerful surroundings and pleasant home-like life." Indeed, such arrangements had advantages—they were economical and convenient and the librarian, being close to her work, could "be located at any time"; however, they also had drawbacks, especially when the librarians had to abide by student curfews.[21]

Dormitory life included meals, an added benefit for those who disliked cooking. Nonetheless, Ida A. Kidder, who lived for many years in a dormitory at the Oregon State Agricultural College, cautioned a prospective employee that "if you were dieting the dormitory would not answer as no exceptions are made except for the temporarily ill." Kidder paid $21.00 monthly for dormitory room and board in 1911

*3.1. Ridenbaugh Hall dormitory room, University of Idaho, ca. 1907.
Courtesy University of Idaho Historical Photograph Collection*

and estimated that a person could take meals elsewhere for an additional five dollars "and get the kind of board you would want."[22]

In colleges with inadequate or nonexistent dormitory housing, librarians and other women faculty found themselves living in cottages or houses with female students. At least one librarian welcomed this responsibility, regarding it as an adventure. She "immediately began to select furniture and all that goes with a house, to interview plumbers, paper-hangers, etc." She had some "good times" with her charges, but expressed concern that she did "not make a very grave and dignified chaperon."[23]

Finally, western librarians discovered that shopping for clothing and food could be quite challenging. Products available locally usually cost more than they did in the East, and library school directors advised prospective librarians to consider the higher cost of clothing and

3.2. *Ridenbaugh Hall dining room, University of Idaho, ca. 1908.*
Courtesy University of Idaho Historical Collection

other supplies before accepting western employment. Belle Sweet encouraged her newly hired assistant librarian to visit a dressmaker before starting West because

> we have very poor dressmakers here and a trip to Spokane
> adds greatly to the cost which is already high. . . . It is also
> well to come with a full supply of shoes especially if you
> wear a medium or narrow width.[24]

In addition to adjusting to the western environment and living conditions, the newly arrived librarians also had to adapt socially. As single professional women, they had few counterparts, especially in rural communities. Library school directors and employers cautioned graduate librarians that positions in the West would require them to be "dependent entirely on their own resources for [social entertainment]" because towns often had "none of the amusements and opportunities afforded by a city." This reality, however, usually came as a shock. In particular, women who moved to rural communities experienced a deep sense of geographic, cultural, and social isolation. Even though they generally described the western people as cordial and supportive, "appreciative" of their efforts, and "always ready to meet strangers at least half way," they nonetheless missed having friends their own age with similar interests. A librarian in Pendleton, Oregon, described residents there:

> Very few of the people are at all literary, although some of
> the club ladies imagine themselves so. Fiction is the reading
> indulged in by the majority of the people, altho [sic] the
> high school is doing very good work.[25]

After spending a year or more in the collegial atmosphere of a library school, it could be difficult to adjust to the idea of living miles from others who shared their enthusiasm for librarianship.

Librarians at western colleges and normal schools had the benefit of like-minded colleagues, most of them male. One of six women on a staff of twenty-seven, Belle Sweet's female colleagues at the University of Idaho included instructors in English, domestic science, and modern languages. She found the men, "together with their wives" to be "delightful friends and acquaintances" and thrived in the "spirit of helpfulness, co-operation and appreciation . . . sometimes lacking in the larger institutions of the East."[26]

In spite of their minority status in western communities, these women seldom commented on the attention they received from men. Mabel Prentiss caught a cold when she visited one California community to organize its library. After being escorted home by the local physician, by way of his office for some medication, she later learned that three councilmen had each boasted that he would see her home: "Well, when I was escorted out by Dr. Thayer and they *all* got left, they had such a laugh on each other that they had to tell the joke to everyone." And when Mabel Wilkinson visited Glendo, Wyoming, she had an interesting experience with several cowpunchers. While dining in Glendo's leading hotel, she heard "hearty laughter" and "joshing" coming from the next room. Soon after, the door opened and "six punchers appeared attired in characteristic soft shirts with the bandanna kerchiefs around the neck, 'chaps', high-heeled boots and jingling spurs." As soon as they spied Wilkinson, however, they fled back into the room "from whence they reappeared about five minutes later

3.3. Moscow, Idaho, Fourth of July parade, 1907.
Courtesy University of Idaho Historical Photograph Collection

with their hair neatly combed; neckties taking the place of the ban-
dannas; coats on; minus the 'chaps', spurs, and rollicking manner.''
She later learned that only two single women lived within a thirty-five
mile radius of the town.[27]

Many women wrote that they felt extremely lonesome or homesick,
and that they missed being around people their own ages or others
who shared the same taste in books, music, and entertainment. A
normal school librarian in Lewiston, Idaho, confided: "You don't
know how I long some times to hear good music and good lectures and
good plays.'' A number of the older women, however, sought consolation in their work. Reporting that her "only lonesome moments are
those which are spent away from the library,'' one woman noted that
she had begun bringing projects home to help her pass the long
evening hours in her room. Those who could not adjust to this en-
forced isolation, however, eventually sought work in more populous

areas: "I hate to think of spending many more months here in such lonliness [*sic*]."[28]

Daily responsibilities, long distances, and weather limited and even precluded many visits with other librarians. Edith Morgan, a normal school librarian in Gunnison, Colorado, knew that long periods of isolation would accompany the snow: "The white legions of the snow are besieging our valley . . . and it will not be long before they will come on down the slopes, to keep us prisoners for many months."[29] The newly appointed librarian in Kalispell, Montana, recognized that it would be difficult to consult with a colleague because her's was the only public library within a 270-mile radius.

With the exception of joining a women's club or church, few of these women mentioned partaking in the local community activities. Lucy Lewis, however, represents an exception. She enjoyed an active social life at the New Mexico College of Agriculture and Mechanic Arts that included "afternoon parties and teas and calls to be made." She found people "quite exacting" and felt compelled to attend their social functions. Dances, held every Saturday night at the dormitory, featured music "furnished by a 'one-man band,' consisting of the only minister in town." Charlotte Baker, who preceded Lewis in Las Cruces, recalled that the young country people enjoyed playing pranks on her—surprising her with snakes, mice, and horned toads—and that some residents considered it "an unpardonable sin" that she could not cook.[30]

Small communities often hired only one librarian, and possibly a part-time assistant or janitor, but in larger communities the library staff included reference librarians, catalogers, loan desk attendants, and other assistants. In these institutions, female librarians often became friends and formed social networks. Some organized book discussion groups and library clubs while others went on picnics and excursions. Five women at the Spokane Public Library founded the Spokane Walking Club in 1915, motivated by their desire for outdoor recreation. By April 1918, they had taken approximately one hundred scheduled walks, some as long as fourteen miles in length.[31]

Many western librarians became emotionally dependent upon frequent correspondence with library school directors to sustain them through difficult times. Directors encouraged their graduates to remain in close contact, especially during the early years of their careers, telling them that they would "always want long letters" and that they expected to have "frequent reports." Graduating from library schools

3.4. Spokane Public Library staff picnic, July 11, 1913.
Courtesy Spokane Public Library

only a year or two before moving West, few of these women had ventured far from home for their first library positions. When they reached the "wild and wooly [*sic*] West," as they sometimes described it, the former students often sent letters immediately—"arrived this morning at 3"—assuring directors that they had safely reached their destination. The ensuing correspondence then evolved into requests for advice, progress reports, and at times indicated a degree of emotional dependence:

> You told me I might write you when I felt like it, and I feel
> quite like it tonight. I miss you so much, your deep
> enthusiasm and unshakeable [*sic*] interest in libraries, your
> good sense, your experience . . . I am just starving to talk to
> somebody who knows and loves librarians . . . I love and
> prize you more every day.[32]

Another woman, anxious "to make good in library work as I did in teaching," described her letter to a library school director as a plea "for help in the hour of my greatest need."[33]

When they received letters written in a highly emotional tone, directors sometimes feared for their graduate's mental stability. After receiving a gushing, adoring letter from a graduate situated in Washington, Katharine L. Sharp cautiously replied: "That was a very nice letter which you wrote to me and I wish that I could answer it in kind."[34] In a separate letter to a colleague, however, Sharp confided that she feared this woman had too strong an emotional side. She sometimes asked other librarians in the vicinity to check up on librarians who appeared, in their letters, to be unstable, even hysterical.

Some women attributed their feelings of depression to boarding house life, especially women who had been used to a wide circle of companions. Others noted, somewhat matter-of-factly, that outside of the landlady, there were no other females living in the house. Lacking companionable conversation, they retired to their rooms where they wrote letters, washed shirt-waists, or continued work they had not been able to finish during the day.

That the directors' interest in and concern for their students helped alleviate homesickness is evident. One woman wrote: "You don't know how much good it did me just to see your handwriting on the envelope." Others regarded letters from library school directors as well-timed "inflators." Graduates appreciated the directors' genuine concern for their welfare, and came to think of themselves as members of the directors' "girls" or "family."[35]

A few graduates expressed reservations about writing because, in their eyes, they had nothing significant to report. Others felt so far removed from what they had learned in library school and, laboring under pioneer conditions, found that they could not manage their libraries according to standard practices. Such circumstances prompted apologies:

> Many a time I have sat me down to write to you, but I've
> been ashamed . . . I haven't accomplished any great
> changes—and I've pretty nearly forgotten the rule of
> thumb! I know how all the other girls have been writing you
> about starting sociology classes, and advertizing in the street
> cars.

Clearly, they felt a sense of responsibility for extending the school's reputation in a new region, and wanted "to do the right thing" as representatives of the school, but at the same time they felt that they needed to be responsible for themselves.[36]

Recognizing that a woman's mood could change drastically between the time she wrote a letter and received a response, library school directors generally advised their graduates to get plenty of rest, to eat well, and to take vacations. While they acknowledged these women's feelings of discouragement, they did not dwell on them:

> I imagine that when you wrote your letter you were feeling a little blue and conditions did not seem very attractive . . . if you do the right kind of work and fit into the Western spirit it will not be long before you have better opportunities.

At times, however, they even chastised those who complained too often: "If you have not enough within yourself or can not get enough from books and from helping people . . . then I have little patience with you." While directors recognized the importance of their correspondence with graduates, it sometimes became difficult to reply promptly because of the great volume of letters they received. The director of the University of Illinois Library School hastened to reassure a student that his "failure to answer your letter after your arrival in the west" was not due to lack of interest but to stress of circumstances.[37]

In giving both encouragement and admonitions, directors helped these women develop personally and professionally. Some may have consciously tried to wean students by encouraging them to enter into local social life and to cultivate friendships with colleagues in the region. Until that occurred, however, library school directors gave unselfishly of their time and knowledge, helping their graduates adjust to western conditions and to life adrift. Over time, a number of these mentoring relationships evolved into warm friendships that transcended professional concerns and endured for many years.

As more professional librarians took up residence in the West, they began to develop collegial networks composed of colleagues employed by the same library, in the same community, or in the same state. In larger libraries, staff meetings sometimes provided a forum for social interaction. One librarian discovered "such a 'homey' spirit at the Public Library of Portland," where they devoted a portion of their bimonthly staff meetings to the discussion of current events and new books.[38] Library director, Mary Frances Isom, opened her home to librarians from around the state for luncheons and other social occasions where librarians could make one another's acquaintance.

In states that had only a few professionally trained librarians, they soon knew when another joined their ranks and they promptly sent words of welcome. Cornelia Marvin made it a practice to visit new librarians in Oregon, providing them words of encouragement as well as practical advice and insight into their new communities. One women, feeling "rather battered, and beaten and bruised" after a difficult period at her library, recalled a visit Marvin had made and "took heart again."[39]

Librarians often visited one another and sometimes even spent their holidays together. Sometimes they planned vacations that consisted of stops at various friends' libraries. Cornelia Marvin and Mary Frances Isom developed a close friendship, spending many weekends together. When some time had elapsed since Marvin's last visit, Isom wrote: "Please let me know when I may expect you and how long you can stay so that I can make my plans and kill the fatted calf." Although distance presented some difficulty, these women sustained each other through correspondence when they could not be together. Marvin also developed a close friendship with Ida Kidder, who would "pour out my heart to you when we have been separated for a long time."[40]

The many western librarians who found themselves in one-person libraries eagerly awaited the day when they could appoint assistants. After Althea Warren organized the San Diego Public Library, she found herself in need of additional help. She wanted to hire a friend to work with her, but she feared that the board would never approve. Librarians wanted to employ professionally trained women, but it became even more important for them to have companionable colleagues. Evidence of loneliness emerges in their letters to library school directors: "I care much more for personality and willingness to work than for technical perfection. Most of all I want someone who is pleasant to work with. . . . Please send me someone nice." Often, when librarians expressed a preference for graduates of their alma maters, it was not because of personal friendship, but because they "would be accustomed to the same rules and it would be easier to work together."[41]

In libraries where professionally educated assistants worked under untrained librarians, conflict sometimes arose. The assistant librarian at the University of Montana accused her untrained director of trying to discredit her with the chancellor. In a letter to Mary E. Hazeltine, she attributed the problem to the librarian's dislike for her. Hazeltine gently chided: "No chief likes to have an assistant appear to do better work than she does herself," and closed by suggesting that the assistant attempt to still the troubled waters by sending flowers or making another "nice" gesture.[42] Such advice would have been of little consolation to a young librarian working in a hostile environment. Fortunately, the majority of the graduates found themselves working with "splendid" women and welcomed the opportunity to work under their direction.

Library school directors expressed delight to see communities of their graduates forming in the West, especially on the Pacific Coast. Such gatherings began to fill the void created as the librarians moved away from the family circle. If employers found satisfaction with a librarian's performance, they tended to contact her alma mater when they decided to recruit additional librarians or to replace her. In some instances, graduates of the same school or class began work together in larger public and academic libraries. A newly appointed librarian at the University of California in Berkeley reported: "Miss Carroll and I started our work here in July, and were especially pleased with our reception." The University of Illinois sponsored regular banquets for alumni in several western cities. While at the Pacific Northwest Library Association meeting in Portland in 1920, Lucy Lewis attended an Illinois Library school dinner one evening and was "surprised that there were so many of us."[43]

State and regional meetings provided opportunities for librarians to renew acquaintances, to exchange ideas with colleagues, to visit other libraries, and to purchase items that were unavailable locally. Not all states, however, had library associations during this period, and geographic barriers and the paucity of library workers in a state made it difficult to schedule regular meetings. A librarian at the State Normal School in Cheney, Washington, considered herself fortunate to be able to attend the state library convention in Spokane, where she had "a fine opportunity" to meet "about fifteen librarians other than the Spokane four in attendance." Elizabeth Ritchie, librarian of the Kalispell, Montana, Public Library, rejoiced when the board granted her "the privilege of attending the State Library Association at Great Falls during the Christmas holidays." And Edith Morgan, librarian of the normal school in Gunnison, Colorado, looked forward to the 1916 meeting of the Colorado Library Association—even though it meant fifteen hours of travel each way—for the "two days of inspiration and information and one of shopping and visiting."[44] Clearly, professional meetings met both professional and personal needs.

~ four ~

Defining a Constituency

Western normal school, college, and university libraries provided the cultural crusaders with an opportunity to extend the library's influence throughout the land. Although the more prestigious universities preferred to appoint male library directors, fledgling institutions, especially those at normal schools and state agricultural colleges, welcomed women librarians.[1] After initiating library service for students and faculty, the women began to find ways that they could extend service to rural readers. The latter represented a population that often lived beyond the jurisdiction of existing municipal public libraries. Thus, in defining their constituency broadly, women academic librarians provided an invaluable service until other agencies—state library commissions, traveling libraries, and county library service—developed to meet these needs.

An 1876 survey listed only seventeen normal school, college, and university libraries in the West, most concentrated along the Pacific Coast (see Table 4.1). The number of colleges increased steadily after the turn of the century, as did the number of students they enrolled. Administrators at some western institutions recognized the desirability of hiring a librarian with professional credentials, but very few actually comprehended the extent of her duties. Many colleges and normal schools had previously relied on professors, bookkeepers, registrars, stenographers, or students to supervise the library on a part-time basis.

For years the president of the Montana State College of Agriculture and Mechanical Arts had placed a student in charge of the library, "not realizing that library work requires special training." The president of the University of Idaho informed that school's first professional librarian that he "knew nothing of library schools." Her appointment was "the first time they had ever been brought to his notice." He

Table 4.1 Colleges, Universities, and Public/Private Normal Schools in the American West, 1876–1916

Region	1876	1890–1	1898–9	1910	1915–16
Pacific Coast	16	36	40	37	42
California	13	20	17	17	24
Oregon	2	9	13	11	9
Washington	1	7	10	9	9
Southwest	0	1	4	8	9
Arizona	0	1	2	3	3
New Mexico	0	0	2	5	6
Rocky Mountain	1	9	22	21	22
Colorado	0	4	6	9	10
Idaho	0	0	3	4	4
Montana	0	1	4	4	4
Nevada	0	1	1	1	1
Utah	1	1	7	2	2
Wyoming	0	2	1	1	1
Total	17	46	66	66	73

Sources: *Public Libraries of the U.S.A.* (Washington, D.C.: Government Printing Office, 1876, pp. 1012–1142; *Report of the Commissioner of Education for the Year 1880* (Washington, D.C.: Government Printing Office, 1882), 2:88–89; *Report of the Commissioner of Education for the Year 1890–91* (Washington, D.C.: Government Printing Office, 1894), 2:1398–1413, 1451–56; *Report of the Commissioner of Education for the Year 1898–99* (Washington, D.C.: Government Printing Office, 1900), 2:1592, 1793, 1801; *Report of the Commissioner of Education for the Year Ended June 30, 1910* (Washington, D.C.: Government Printing Office, 1911), 2:853, 1080; and *Report of the Commissioner of Education for the Year Ended June 30, 1917* (Washington, D.C.: Government Printing Office, 1918), 2:295, 447, 454.

wanted a library school graduate, however, because he "went in for specialized work in all departments."[2]

Uncertainty about the librarian's status within the campus community also created confusion about her salary and vacation—should it be equal to other faculty? The president of the state normal school in Gunnison, Colorado, decided to award his librarian the same amount of vacation time as the teaching faculty received, but his wife objected, claiming that librarians in other schools "took the same vacations as the clerks and stenographers." Librarian Edith Morgan stood her ground: "I courteously explained to her that library work . . . , only

4.1. The library in Old Main (McFie Hall), New Mexico College of Agriculture and Mechanic Arts, ca. 1904–09.
Courtesy of Hobson-Huntsinger University Archives, New Mexico State University Library

lately having come to be considered a profession, is slowly coming to its own.'' In many institutions, administrators assigned the librarian a variety of additional duties. When Charlotte A. Baker arrived at the New Mexico State College of Agriculture and Mechanic Arts in 1900, her responsibilities included supervising the library, ringing the bell for classes, selling stationery to the community, running the local mail distribution center, teaching English to preparatory classes, and helping with college entertainments. Baker later boasted that she shed some of her extra duties by purposely forgetting them.[3]

Textbook distribution represented another time-consuming and frustrating activity assigned to some of these librarians. Administrators assigned them this responsibility because the library had organized machinery for book buying. One woman vented her anger and frustration with textbook distribution responsibilities:

If there is anything that is trying, it is this text-book library.
We would get a person all fitted out with books and then he

would change his course. My reason was nearly gone when
the work was over.[4]

A number of administrators expected librarians to teach—often
courses in English as well as in library use—perhaps because many of
the librarians' predecessors had been professor-librarians. Women
who had taken up library work after leaving careers in teaching occasionally expressed dismay upon learning that they would again have to
maintain order in a classroom. Gladys Germand, describing her teaching responsibilities at the University of Wyoming, lamented: "It is not
an honor which I have sought, oh no, but one that has been thrust
upon me." Fenimore Schwartz, initially delighted with her appointment at the University of Washington Library, had reservations after
hearing that librarians also had to teach courses in the library school:
"I have been looking forward to this work . . . but all of the pleasure
is gone now if I have to teach and only dread is left."[5]
     At some schools the appointment of a trained librarian repre-
sented a symbol of progress. Charlotte Baker recalled somewhat wryly
that her school's president

> used to exhibit me to visitors when I first went down [to Las
> Cruces] as a *trained librarian*. If I only could have had a
> string tied to my belt and a hand-organ to dance to the
> illusion would have been complete.[6]

Faculty, eager to see their libraries become "thoroughly up to date,"
usually supported their librarians enthusiastically. Belle Sweet reflected:

> Everyone connected with the university [of Idaho] seems to
> have realized that the library was not in good condition and
> each one seems to be anxious to do whatever is possible . . .
> in order to help me.

Students also appreciated improved conditions in the library. Those at
the University of Idaho wished that Sweet had arrived several years
earlier: "Then we could have found something when we wanted it."
Elizabeth Forrest received similar support at Montana State College,

where the faculty "practically forced my employment in order to have improved cataloging and reference work."[7]

Even after appointing professional librarians, however, some administrators remained reluctant to delegate any significant degree of authority. One woman complained that her principal's fiat determined "whether or not we shall buy books . . . what magazines we shall take." Some resented not being allowed to communicate directly to the board of regents. Lucy Lewis expressed discouragement that her requests to the regents of the New Mexico College of Agriculture and Mechanic Arts "did not reach the Board in the same form" as she had submitted them. Lewis concluded that she was the victim of "political 'wires' and influences."[8]

Newly appointed western academic librarians frequently compared established eastern universities with pioneer western schools, most of which appeared to be experiencing rapid, and seemingly unplanned, growth. When Lucy Lewis arrived in Las Cruces in 1906, she learned that "our enrollment is the largest it has ever been." Nonetheless, unstable economic conditions and the impermanence of university administrators affected her school and its library adversely.

Criticism of presidents and their fiscal management appeared repeatedly in the librarians' letters to friends and colleagues. Many felt no sense of permanence because of the frequency with which administrative turnover occurred. A librarian in Washington observed in 1904 that "presidents change so rapidly and policies are so varied, that except as a stepping stone, one would not crave this." Women at state-supported schools felt especially vulnerable because their schools appeared subject to merger at any moment. When E. A. Bryan tendered his resignation as president of Washington State College in 1910, a librarian there wrote that things looked "rather blue" because "agitation grows toward the consolidation of the two state schools." Constant turnover also meant that a president who supported the library could easily be replaced by one with different priorities. After one supportive administrator left the State Normal School in Cheney, Washington, Katherine Kiemle found the new principal's attitude toward the library disturbing—"one of indifference, and I feel as tho [sic] I had no patron saint to whom I can turn."[9]

State legislators, responsible for allocating funds for western schools, appeared to have little appreciation for or understanding of colleges, universities, and normal schools, even less for libraries. Although Belle Sweet expected great things to happen in Idaho, she became disillusioned when the "Senate and our Governor became possessed of the idea that a university is a luxury and anyway it does not need support." After they allocated less money to the university in 1915 than it had received during the previous biennium, another Idaho librarian prayed for the election of a Republican governor, observing that it would be difficult to predict the future "if the Democrat candidate continues." Her prayers went unanswered, however, and the regents terminated her school's cataloging project as one of several economy measures.[10]

Fiscal uncertainty led some college presidents and normal school principals to employ irregular practices in order to keep their institutions open. A librarian in the Southwest expressed dismay at the variety of ways that she had seen Morrill Act money for the support of land-grant colleges and universities being used. Another, working at a normal school in Lewiston, Idaho, confided that her institution's president was in serious difficulty for overspending and had attempted "to get around the law some way in order to keep running." Few western institutions had enough money to allocate for library books, furniture, facilities, or the librarian's salary. The principal of the New Mexico College of Agriculture and Mechanic Arts denied all requests for salary increases "owing to a temporary financial stringency largely due to lack of foresight on the part of the retiring president."[11] This led Lewis to question whether eastern schools conducted business in this manner or if it was "only the wild west carrying high finance into state institutions."[12]

Enthusiastic, energetic, and eager to make the academic library an agency of influence and uplift, the graduate librarians began by organizing their disorderly legacy. They evidently accepted Dewey's maxim that an efficient library—one with orderly books and well-behaved and well-trained users—is an effective library. Soon after her arrival in Las Cruces, Lucy Lewis wrote that she had found "such a field for the work" that it made her "shiver and gasp." Doris Greene, however, believed that pioneer conditions might be too overwhelming for recent graduates. She concluded, after one month at the University of Wyoming, that it was "no place to send a girl just out of library school." Others shared similar reactions. Soon after her arrival at the University of Idaho in 1916, Julia Stockett informed the preceptress of the Wisconsin Library School that "even you Miss Hazeltine, would be a little

*4.2. "Literary laboratory," Greeley, Colorado, 1895.
Courtesy University of Northern Colorado Archives*

downhearted at times over the condition of this library." In such instances, however, librarians expressed appreciation that library school
faculty had taught them "how to make the best of the situation when
conditions were not ideal."[13]

Discipline became a major question for many, in part because a
number of western institutions offered preparatory classes to compensate students for inadequate high school preparation. Librarians expressed concern about discipline because the library often doubled as
the college's only study hall. Lucy Lewis observed that the students in
Las Cruces were "very young," making the question of discipline and
order an important issue. The president and members of the library
committee warned her to expect a great deal of trouble: "They related
to me tales of how students had had to be sent form [*sic*] the library for
'rough housing' . . . breaking the furniture, and so forth." As a result,
she went to the library her first morning "with visions of myself forcibly
ejecting some brawny six footer, out of the library, by the coat collar."
A report issued in New Mexico in 1909, indicating that few schools in
the territory could carry pupils beyond the eighth grade, in part ex-

4.3. *Grace Raymond Hebard in the University of Wyoming Library.*
Courtesy Grace Raymond Hebard Collection (#8), American Heritage Center,
University of Wyoming

plains this situation. [14] A librarian at the Montana State College attributed her initial problems with discipline to the fact that her predecessor had been more "policeman than librarian." Another struggled because before her arrival the library had been "a joke—a place for flirtation and fun." Ida Kidder, however, had no problem maintaining "excellent discipline" at Oregon State Agricultural College. An observer there attributed Kidder's success to either her "unusual powers of pouring oil on troubled waters, or to the angelic disposition of Oregon youth." [15]

Academic librarians typically found their libraries housed in a room, or rooms, within another college building, and they often constituted the sole staff. The University of Wyoming housed its thirty-six thousand volumes "in five rooms of the liberal arts building," while in New Mexico Lucy Lewis had a "main library consisting of Loan department, reference department, reading room, work room, stack room, and conversation room, *all in one room.*" Nearly all of the western librarians expressed eagerness to have new quarters and, ultimately,

4.4. University Library and Museum, Tucson, Arizona, erected 1903.
Courtesy American Library Association Archives

separate library buildings but, again, western economic conditions slowed their progress. After New Mexico legislators allocated money for a college library building in 1908, a discouraged Lewis reported that "owing to lack of funds . . . they cut down the size of my rooms so much that I fear they will have to move the library again in a very few years." Numerous other setbacks occurred elsewhere. Bonds issued in 1906 for a library building at the University of Montana were declared illegal, leading that institution's librarian to conclude: "It will be years before any advancements can be made."[16]

In 1900, only three western institutions had free-standing library buildings—Colorado College, Mills College, and the University of California. During the next twenty years only five additional buildings would be constructed—at the University of Denver, Oregon State Agricultural College, Pomona College, Stanford University, and the University of Utah. Ida Kidder recognized the significance of her success in securing a library building for the Oregon State Agricultural College in 1911:

> Have you seen the June *Library Journal* with the beautiful
> pictures of my library as frontispiece? I am very proud of it
> and glad to have the librarians of the country know that we
> are progressing out here in the wild and woolly west.[17]

Defining a Constituency ∼ 67

Buildings, however, represent only one measure of achievement. Before western academic librarians could develop outreach programs—collections of books sent to country schools, reference work for citizens of the state—they had to gain control of the collections they inherited. Cataloging and classification became an immediate priority because most collections had never been completely and systematically organized. Ida Kidder's predecessor at the Oregon State Agricultural College had carried the catalog in his head; after his departure it became virtually impossible to locate specific titles. At the New Mexico College of Agriculture and Mechanic Arts, Charlotte Baker's predecessor had kept books behind a counter. Students selected their reading material by leaning over to see which ones looked the most worn, associating wear with interesting and useful content.

When Mabel Shrum became librarian at the Colorado School of Mines in 1901, she found her library in great confusion. Not only did the books lack book numbers but also they had "no labels on the outside so there is no kind of order on the shelves." Professors there hoarded books in special locations so they could find them when needed. Books at the University of Idaho had scattered across the campus during the absence of a full-time librarian. No record of them existed, and one of the librarian's first actions was to retrieve the books and rearrange the library, a project that she knew would not inconvenience students because "very few . . . know where to find things any way."[18]

Many encountered disheveled piles of government documents that proliferated with astounding regularity, and few librarians knew how to organize them. They often stored documents in closets, basements, or any other available space until a request for information necessitated that they be retrieved. After storing documents "on the vacant shelves and on the floor and any place where there happened to be room," a University of Idaho librarian concluded that it was "absolutely impossible to find anything that is wanted."[19]

Even in institutions that had previously employed itinerant catalogers, the collections had fallen into disarray through use and as the collection grew. After the itinerant librarian's departure, others attempted to continue the work with varying degrees of success. A public librarian from Butte, who "cataloged according to no accepted system," had organized the Montana State College library. After his departure a woman with only the first year of a country high school education, various members of the faculty, and even the college president attempted to carry on the work.[20]

Lack of adequate funds made it difficult, if not impossible, for the librarian to secure assistance. As a result, graduate librarians spent endless hours doing menial tasks. Roxana Johnson urged officials at Washington State College to provide her with some relief from mechanical routine, arguing that a stenographer should be performing the clerical aspects of library work: "It seems such a waste of time for me to have to alphabet cards, match the L.C. cards to books, etc."[21] Johnson's request, no matter how persuasive, could not be granted.

Lacking assistance, librarians often became immersed in and overwhelmed by technical duties. Finding it impossible to accomplish everything during regular work hours, they began working evenings and weekends. A Montana librarian reported spending all of her "Friday and Saturday nights in the Library . . . reading shelves, classifying and doing odds and ends that were left over."[22] After two years at the Montana State College, a tired and discouraged Elizabeth Forrest summed up her limited progress:

> So far I have accomplished almost nothing . . . I am still
> cataloging without a type-writer, have a scanty and out of
> date reference collection . . . the public documents in an
> overcrowded closet in the basement, have money to bind
> only 87 out of 159 periodicals . . . and have literally not
> even floor space to collect experimental station bulletins.[23]

Library school faculty advised their graduates to avoid becoming too bogged down in detailed, mechanical work, believing that librarians should establish themselves as a presence in the community:

> I do not question at all the need of a thorough revision [of
> the cataloging], but when you are so new in a community, it
> would seem to us that your best move right now is to get
> acquainted with your public, and to do that you would need
> to be pretty constantly in the public eye.[24]

Dust, pests, and fire represented just a few additional impediments to the western librarian's work. In her annual reports to the president of the University of Wyoming, Grace Raymond Hebard documented

4.5. Colorado Agricultural College Library, Christmas, 1915.
Courtesy Colorado State University Archives

her continual battle with pests and odors. The manure spread on the university grounds served as "an excellent breeding place" for mice and flies:

> This year the mice have followed the pipes and entered the
> library through the too large holes . . . eating the backs off
> of the pamphlets to get the glue. The Librarian has
> superintended the killing of these pests the best she could
> from the top of the chair and on the table.

Hebard and her staff spent their "spare time swatting the flies" and worrying about the gasoline fumes that wafted into the library through the unscreened windows, concerned because "gasoline and books have no affinity." And during winters in Fort Collins, Colorado, Charlotte Baker battled frozen pipes: "I put a paper torch in a stove pipe elbow and trotted up and down the pipes for an hour and a half thawing them out. It was smoky, and I shed real tears."[25]

Fire posed an ever-present threat for early schools with their wood-

4.6. Library in men's gymnasium, University of Idaho, ca. 1906–07.
Courtesy University of Idaho Historical Photograph Collection

frame buildings and wood or coal stoves. In the spring of 1906 the University of Idaho lost its administrative building and the library contained within. Although the "dreadful calamity at Stanford and at California"—the 1906 earthquake—made her own loss "seem small in comparison," University of Idaho librarian Belle Sweet nonetheless mourned the nearly twelve thousand volumes consumed by fire. During her short tenure at the university (she had arrived the previous fall), Sweet had added nearly fifteen hundred dollars worth of new books—all except those in circulation had burned. For lack of better space, Sweet reopened the library on the main floor of the gymnasium and, with a typewriter and some postage, began sending appeals for donations to authors, colleagues, and publishers. The approximately 340 individuals she contacted included such prominent women as Jane Addams and M. Carey Thomas. Sweet and other librarians, who suffered losses due to fires, earthquakes, or other disasters, appreciated the support given by their eastern colleagues. Offers of assistance included copies of library school class notes, manuals, and supplies.[26]

Administrators assured Sweet that she would soon have new quarters, but a year later the library and the gymnasium continued to share space because of a delay in the receipt of the insurance check. Sweet described the "lightning change" that occurred at four every day when the library reverted to a gymnasium:

> A hundred chairs disappear behind the book cases and the tables form a pyramid equal to any ever seen in a circus. . . . You can imagine the dust, noise and confusion but this is not all. All mass meetings, basket-ball games and musicale recitals are held here.[27]

Working in this "temporary" facility, Sweet struggled to restore order while maintaining her dedication to service.

Given such conditions, western academic librarians found themselves departing from the ideal practices they had learned in library school. Working alone, and with inadequate supplies, they took short cuts in the mechanical work in order to create time for work with the public. The extent of their departure from standard practice became especially evident when newly minted graduate librarians replaced them during leaves of absence or after they resigned. When Mabel Reynolds prepared to take a year's leave of absence from the Washington State Normal School in Cheney she expressed reservations about having a library school graduate replace her:

> The difficulty with a Library School worker as I see it would be her impatience at doing things at such variance to library school rules . . . I have modified and modified; there is so much to be done and I have learned how much to omit by experience.[28]

After attaining some measure of order in their libraries, even when it meant taking short-cuts, western academic librarians could turn their energies to extension work. Soon after her arrival at the University of Idaho in 1906 Belle Sweet observed: "There certainly is a chance for a great deal of missionary work in this part of the country and I hope to be able to do something to help things along."[29] Pioneer conditions had not dulled her desire, instilled during library school days, to extend the library's influence throughout the community and the state.

Sweet, and many others, took their responsibility to the citizens of the state seriously, especially in states that had limited public library service. The librarian of the Colorado State Agricultural College library articulated this sentiment in 1902, stating that "in the absence of other agencies" the agricultural college library could "do a great deal for the rural teacher and the ranchman or farmer." State normal school and agricultural college libraries circulated traveling libraries to many rural communities, and librarians found in farmers' and teachers' institutes a forum for publicizing their services. Wyoming residents began looking to the University of Wyoming for traveling libraries, and Grace Raymond Hebard "constantly, daily, many times a day" prepared individual books or packages of books "to be sent to schools, granges, women's clubs, and community Sunday Schools."[30]

In the absence of public libraries, western residents turned to nearby normal school, college, and university libraries for services as well as for books. Academic librarians provided study outlines for women's clubs and sent duplicate periodicals to lumber and mining camps. In 1912, Charlotte Baker and her assistants at the Colorado State Agricultural College traveled on an agricultural exhibit train that visited rural communities. They also sent package libraries to county agents, and used vacation time to help local public libraries and schools organize their collections. Not every academic library, however, had the equipment or funds to support traveling library work. An Illinois graduate in charge of the Montana State Agricultural College library wanted to provide similar service, but concluded: "Before we can do extension work in this library we will have to have something to extend."[31]

By providing library service to country teachers, western academic librarians reached a community of readers that extended well beyond the college campus. Moreover, they planted the seeds of support for the public and school libraries. Edith Morgan, a normal school librarian, recalled:

> During my first year, the routine work took more time than
> it usually requires; the next year there was more time for
> giving the teachers and students individual reference help,
> assisting rural school teachers . . . in an effort to make it
> impossible for them to get along without good school
> libraries.[32]

Teachers, in turn, shared their books—and an interest in reading—with their students, who often took them home for use by other family members. Some campuses provided service directly to country homes. Morgan initiated a books-by-mail service, circulating books by parcel post from the State Normal School in Gunnison. She knew that ultimately a county system would develop, but in the interim families living within a reasonable distance of her school would have books. Other librarians, recognizing that rural teachers had little time to read and evaluate books, prepared buying lists of recommended titles to assist them in developing school libraries.[33]

Over time, other library workers and trustees began turning to the academic librarians for assistance. As "authorities" on library work, academic librarians could influence public library development. A cataloger at the University of Oregon used her position as chair of the local Fortnightly Club's Library Extension Committee to "increase the efficiency of the public library" in Eugene.[34] In Gunnison, Colorado, Edith Morgan demonstrated her public spirit by "starting a Public Reading Room movement when little or no interest in this movement existed."[35]

Other western academic librarians traveled the region giving inspirational talks in local communities to raise public awareness of and support for the public library movement. Gertrude Buckhous, at the University of Montana, gave "frequent advice with regard to the establishment of small libraries" as did Ida Kidder, librarian of the Oregon State Agricultural College. The latter could not forget her days as a public library organizer, and believed that the college library "should do all that is reasonable and within its power to stimulate the public library in its work for the state." In addition to serving on the Corvallis Public Library Board, she used every occasion she could find "to promote good reading habits by giving lectures to clubs, granges, and other civic organizations."[36] After one such occasion, when she had given "some of the vicious literature such as *Cosmopolitan* and other vile and trashy magazines a good rap," Ida Kidder concluded that local clubs did good work even though some members remained "ignorant of the importance of carefully selecting the reading for their children."[37] Kidder took great care to treat her audiences with respect:

> I did not let them know for a moment that I had ever heard
> anything to their discredit and, any way, I believe in
> Michelangelo's method of reforming people. He said "I
> criticize by creation, not by finding fault."

~ 74 ~

4.7. *Grace Raymond Hebard and Te-ah-win-nil on Shoshone Reservation, September 5, 1926. Courtesy Grace Raymond Hebard Collection (#8), American Heritage Center, University of Wyoming*

The librarian's true mission, she firmly believed, was to reach and to influence as many people as possible. Indeed, she felt "blessed . . . to have a great work to do."[38]

Some academic librarians worked with local library boards to identify candidates for library positions. A few even found themselves spearheading movements to found or revitalize state library associations. Arizona's Estelle Lutrell and Wyoming's Grace Raymond Hebard served their state associations as early officers, while Charlotte Baker restored the Colorado Library Association to its earlier vigor.

Because library schools developed slowly in the West, the library courses offered at western normal schools, colleges, and universities, became the sole form of library training received by a large number of public and school librarians. In addition to instructing students, who in turn would become teacher-librarians, some academic librarians provided private instruction for local librarians in the fundamentals of library work. Lessons typically focused on cataloging, classification, and book selection. A few librarians also provided correspondence study and apprentice-style training for practitioners, but summer school instruction in the fundamentals of library work became the most successful format. The latter appealed to many untrained local women who wished to upgrade but who could ill afford to attend eastern library schools for an entire year.

Recognizing that many University of Wyoming graduates would become country teachers, Grace Raymond Hebard embraced the idea of having "the library interests of the state center around the University Library." A graduate of the Wisconsin Library School who worked with Hebard described that institution's summer library course as "makeshift," but concluded that "in a state where library training stands so little above the zero mark, it seems to me there is real need of such a course until a better one can be offered."[39]

Occasionally administrators encouraged librarians to begin courses in library use before they had finished organizing their collections. Some librarians stalled because they believed it was important to have a model laboratory, but others had no choice but to obey. Only a few months after losing her library to fire, for example, Belle Sweet reluctantly agreed to the president's request that she offer such a course. Some college presidents also encouraged librarians to conduct correspondence study in library science. Uncertain about how to proceed, or whether they should, western academic librarians contacted library schools requesting advice. One feared that it was a poor idea— "There are so few organized libraries which could be used as laboratories"—so she asked a library school director to provide a letter that she could show her president to prove that such a "correspondence course isn't practical."[40]

The academic librarians' library instruction ranged from a series of chapel talks designed to interest students in "good" reading, to a course in children's literature, to a series of library lectures supplemented by practical experience in the library. In an institution with limited funds for student assistants, library courses supplied inexpensive student labor and at the same time exposed students to the rudiments of library work. Librarians derived great satisfaction from watching students use their newly organized libraries. Theodora Brewitt could hardly contain her pride when she watched her "students flock to the catalog even in its incomplete state." She often overheard them explaining the library and its services to the uninitiated. Even administrators began to consider "it [the course in library use] one of the most valuable courses in the school."[41]

Fearing that eastern library schools would think they were competing for students, graduates hastened to assure directors that they did not intend "to start a library school or to grant certificates or degrees for this work." Although their primary goal was to familiarize students with the library and to teach them how to locate information, the knowledge and skills these academic librarians imparted to college students did have a far greater impact. The librarian at a normal school in Colorado offered "a course in 'Library Science' designed to prepare teachers to take charge of their school libraries." Concerned that faculty at the University of Illinois Library School might think poorly of "people gaining a superficial knowledge of the work," she explained that such instruction was necessary in the West where "most country teachers and many city teachers have libraries to administer, and have no better means of learning library work."[42]

~ five ~

Bringing Books and People Together

Describing librarians as "irrepressible expansionists," American Library Association president Ernest C. Richardson announced that the 1905 annual meeting would be held in Portland, Oregon, "for the avowed purpose of doing what could be done to promote the extension of libraries in the Northwest" and for "pushing out the library frontiers."[1] Western states had the beginnings of academic libraries, but much remained to be done before public and school libraries would flourish there.

In 1905, thirty-two-year-old Cornelia Marvin left her position at the Wisconsin Free Library Commission to become the first secretary of the Oregon State Library Commission. She joined Mary Frances Isom, who had journeyed west a few years earlier. Isom, daughter of a Cleveland, Ohio, physician, had lost her mother at an early age. Devoted to her father, she entered library school only after his death, graduating at the age of thirty-six. In May 1901, she accepted an invitation to catalog the holdings of the Library Association of Portland, and shortly afterward, she became that library's first professionally trained librarian. Viewing Oregon as a fertile field for library work, Isom joined forces with the State Federation of Women's Clubs, under the leadership of Sarah Evans, in an effort to create a state library commission. Their campaign succeeded, and in 1905 the state legislature established the Oregon State Library Commission and passed a school library law.

Determined that Oregon's Commission would succeed, Isom traveled to the offices of the Wisconsin Free Library Commission for ad-

5.1. *Cornelia Marvin, July 1905.*
Courtesy Oregon State Library

vice, and while there met with commission worker Cornelia Marvin. The Oregon commission would have only one paid employee—a secretary (in reality, a very powerful position)—and Isom recognized the importance of selecting an individual who possessed vision, leadership abilities, knowledge of library work, and familiarity with the West. Isom found it difficult to believe that Marvin could be interested in the position.[2]

Soon after her return to Portland, however, Isom received a letter followed by a telegram, both emphasizing the seriousness of Marvin's intent and her willingness to take a six-hundred-dollar reduction in salary. Isom, stunned, but overjoyed, replied immediately:

> Your telegram quite took me off my feet, the idea that you could possibly consider the position for yourself never once

occurred to me . . . I feel that the possibilities are really great out here and if we could have you—well, I am speechless. Everything is needed in library work out here . . . and nothing done—libraries and library training and library sentiment all to be created.

In a subsequent letter, Isom again emphasized her eagerness to work with Marvin: "*Do* come—You simply must come and I am sure you will be glad of it." Although the work would be hard and uphill, Isom expressed confidence that Marvin would succeed, and that she would enjoy making the work "hers."[3]

Like many of the Progressive-Era social reformers, Marvin believed that libraries had the power to eradicate ignorance, foster good government, and create responsible, intelligent citizens. Marvin's interest in social and political reform had developed as early as her library school days at the Armour Institute of Technology in Chicago. There she and some classmates set up home libraries in the stockyard slums, meeting Jane Addams and Florence Kelley in the process. Katharine L. Sharp, the library school's director, instilled in Marvin and other protégées a conviction that there was no line of work "more absorbing" than librarianship; indeed, Sharp believed that it was "second only to the church in its possibilities for good."[4]

Marvin's subsequent experiences in Wisconsin, the "laboratory of democracy," during the governorship of Robert M. LaFollette further fostered her desire to provide widespread access to library materials. She enjoyed many elements of her work at the Wisconsin Free Library Commission, but nonetheless had grown restless and discontented as the missionary phase began to be replaced by bureaucracy and politics.[5] Not only did the Oregon position represent an opportunity for pioneer work, but also it carried with it a greater degree of autonomy and a chance for Marvin to develop and implement programs and policies without interference. An additional factor influencing her decision may have been her family's earlier migration to Tacoma, Washington, and her familiarity with that region.

Not everyone greeted the news of Marvin's new position with the same degree of enthusiasm. Sharp recognized that she did not display the "proper missionary spirit" when she confided in Marvin her "personal feeling of regret" that instead of enjoying the results of her earlier efforts, Marvin "should again be doing this hard pioneer work." There existed, as Mary E. Hazeltine would write years later, a distinction between pioneer spirit and missionary spirit, and while many were in sympathy with the work, not every librarian felt herself equal to pioneer conditions that existed in the West.[6]

At the time of Marvin's appointment, Colorado, Idaho, and Washington had state library commissions, but none employed professionally trained librarians. Utah legislators would not pass library commission legislation until 1907, and even then it would serve two functions as the Utah Library Gymnasium Commission. They believed that the gymnasium component would appeal to boys who had not yet formed the reading habit. Meanwhile, the state librarians of California and Washington had high visibility, but neither had formal library training. Thus, it was only natural that library workers in much of the Pacific Northwest looked to Marvin for direction, advice, and training. Almost immediately upon her arrival in Salem, J. M. Hitt, Washington's State Librarian, appealed to her for assistance:

> I am so anxious to do just the right things in building up
> library interests in this state, and not constructing work that
> may later need tearing down that it makes me distrustful of
> myself. . . . Now while you are located in Oregon may we
> not consider that you belong to the Pacific Northwest and
> thus look to you for counsel?

Additionally, Hitt invited Marvin to make an inspection tour of his state's libraries, but Marvin, undoubtedly preoccupied with her own agenda, let a month pass before she declined. She did agree, however, to collaborate on a library bulletin and on some form of library training. Her first course of action, however, was to establish a statewide system of traveling libraries.[7]

Concern for rural readers was not unique to the West. Although traveling libraries existed in America during the early nineteenth century, it was not until 1893, when Melvil Dewey circulated traveling libraries in New York, that the movement gained momentum. While some think that he modeled his plan on the Australian example, others believe that Dewey may have been inspired by the aggressive methods of people who drove mobile chapels through the sparsely settled western country, or by those who transported hives of bees throughout California. Their missionary spirit appealed to Dewey who, along with

5.2. *Traveling library cases.*
Courtesy Idaho State Historical Society

other educators of the era, believed that free access to books would positively influence children and contribute to "the marvelous evolution of the race."[8] Moreover, librarians and educators sought ways to stem the increasing movement of young men and women from the country to the city. Books seemed to be one answer.

A number of turn-of-the-century developments enabled the traveling library movement to thrive. As rapid change threatened to weaken churches and family life, and old-fashioned schools seemed increasingly powerless, educational reformers looked for alternative methods of teaching morality and good citizenship. Librarians, club women, educators, and the public quickly adopted this approach to achieving "the best reading for the largest number at the least cost." Collections of thirty to one-hundred volumes in sturdy trunks (that doubled as bookcases) soon traveled by rail, livery, stage, and boat to library stations located in lumber camps, general stores, post offices, schools, and sod houses throughout the nation.

State traveling library commission members encouraged local communities to form library associations and to elect one from their number to serve as custodian, or librarian, of the traveling library case. These local "librarians" ranged from school masters to merchants to mothers, and worked in tandem with the state library officials to cultivate library spirit within communities. In many remote areas the traveling library was the "most striking evidence of the existence of a state government."[9] A reader in Fruitland, Idaho, went even further:

> Libraries were once luxuries but in this day and age, they
> are better and cheaper than reform schools and
> penitentiaries and are real means of government. They
> belong to our cheapest and best police force. Give us . . .
> more good books and the question of economy will be
> solved.[10]

While library commissions, state libraries, and philanthropists established numerous traveling libraries, club women provided the primary impetus for the movement in many areas. State by state, as they federated, women's clubs expressed an interest in promoting the work, and often raised the necessary funds to support it. Mary Grenning Mitchell, of Great Falls, Montana, wrote: "We want to take the work up, having just formed a State Federation of Clubs."[11] Individual women's clubs sometimes spearheaded the effort, as did the Woman's Columbian Club of Boise and the California Woman's Club, both of which had traveling libraries in circulation as early as 1899.

Club women also lobbied for legislation to ensure the continuance of their traveling library systems, but found legislators reluctant to create new commissions and levy additional taxes. Even though Colorado club women campaigned successfully for legislation to establish a traveling library commission, the state withheld its appropriation for several years. Politics also slowed progress in Idaho, where the governor appointed the secretary of the traveling library commission. As election time approached, and citizens anticipated a Republican administration, a friend suggested that perhaps Mrs. Dockery (Secretary of the Traveling Library Commission) could "flop" and hold her job. When it appeared that the newly elected governor planned to keep his campaign promise to abolish the Idaho Free Library Commission, club women gathered signatures on petitions in the hope that they could prevent this "backward step." While these and similar obstacles retarded the movement's growth, by 1904 club women claimed credit for the development of traveling library service in at least thirty-one states.[12]

*5.3. Cornelia Marvin's first organizing trip, ca. 1905–06.
Courtesy Oregon State Library*

Oregon, with its great distances and sparsely settled communities, became an ideal field for the traveling library work that Cornelia Marvin moved quickly to inaugurate. Marvin planned to serve both children and adults, believing as she did that intervention in the form of wholesome reading material would prevent young men from frequenting the saloons, pool halls, and "blind pigs" prevalent in many western towns. In neighboring California, library workers discovered that a Modesto woman's club had opened a pool room, with a traveling library as a minor feature, in order to keep boys away from the saloons.[13] Many believed that young men would much prefer to read books than to pass their evenings in bars and other "vile" places.

Librarians also promoted the traveling library as an aid to settlement, arguing that access to books would make it easier for settlers to tolerate isolation and adversity. Nebraska Library organizer Edna Bullock, reflecting on the work of the Idaho Library Commission, observed:

When I think of the dull, dusty, remorseless monotony of life in that awful desert, it seems a crime for the state to let

5.4. Wallace Fire Department and Library, Wallace, Idaho.
Courtesy Barnard-Stockbridge Collection, University of Idaho

those who are bold enough to exterminate the sage brush and live in exile (that's what life in southern Idaho looks like to me) to make that desert blossom live without books. The state owes them something for having courage to stay there.[14]

Proof of the work's effectiveness came in the form of letters from children and adults. A local librarian in Bay City, Oregon, assured Marvin that she was using traveling library books to "keep the Boys from the Reform school." She also boasted that the "Bad Boys a round town" who had "bin brakin windows and doing all kinds of Mischief and damage" now came to the library. A young boy in Eastern Oregon claimed that his community no longer needed a curfew law [after they got the traveling library] because the boys "had something good to read at night and they were willing to stay at home." School houses became traveling library stations for a number of reasons. Librarians

5.5. Men eating in bull pen, Kellogg, Idaho, 1897.
Courtesy Barnard Stockbridge Photograph Collection, Univesity of Idaho

could target a particular audience—children—and through the school they could adopt a paternalistic stance in communities with large illiterate populations.[15]

Traveling library workers also received letters from unemployed men who wanted to acquire reading material to help them pass the time. A Washington laborer confided that the market had gone to pieces after the sawmill had shut down. He and his colleagues had been left stranded in "a lonesome place" with "nothing to do but walk around, watch the mill, eat and sleep."[16] Sending lumber men, millworkers, railroad workers, and migrant laborers interesting reading materials became a high priority in many areas. Not only did library workers believe that reading would prevent them from drinking, but they also thought access to books and magazines might trigger a spark within each man that would enable him to lead a better life.

During the early stages of traveling library work, commission workers urged local librarians to push certain classes of reading, often to no avail. A number of traveling library workers relied on the recommended titles mentioned in *Booklist* to compile balanced and high-

*5.6. Reading room, Bunker Hill Mining Company, Idaho.
Courtesy Idaho State Historical Society*

quality collections. "Fixed" collections having something in each for
every age and every taste predominated. Often, however, readers considered these collections too focused, inappropriate, or too scholarly.
An Oregon resident informed Marvin: "I don't beleive [*sic*] people out
here are much interested in the Civil War—you know many of the old
settlers came west to escape taking part in it." When library workers
persisted in circulating such wholesome and educational works as *The
Story of a Grain of Wheat, Cereals in America,* and *Bacteria in Relation to
Country Life,* readers let them languish on the shelves. A farmer concluded that "folks down to the State House think because I'm a farmer
I want to spend my nights reading about fertilizers." The custodian of
a traveling library in a Washington community, after requesting lighter
literature, noted that "our 'sod busters' are not as a rule of the Daniel
Webster type of brain."[17]

The public's seemingly unquenchable thirst for fiction troubled
many turn-of-the-century librarians. Melvil Dewey initially had limited
the amount of fiction contained in New York's traveling libraries to 30

percent, and in 1905 tried to hold it to 50 percent, acknowledging that "our libraries are useless unless they are read." If it was any consolation, Dewey observed, the novels selected by librarians would be far superior to the most widely circulated newspapers. In response to reader requests, Marvin changed Oregon's traveling libraries from "fixed" sets of recommended titles to libraries tailored to meet the interests and needs of individual communities. Based on voluminous correspondence with and visits to residents throughout the state, Marvin labeled the recommended lists as elitist publications compiled by "a university community of educated, cultured people" who sometimes forgot that "people who used traveling libraries are untrained readers."[18]

Advocates of the movement also regarded the traveling library as a vehicle to spread the public library idea to readers living in communities where the soil was not yet conducive to public library development. Librarians believed that the mere presence of a traveling library created a desire within residents for permanent collections of books. Even after communities had established permanent libraries, many continued to supplement their collections with traveling libraries— foreign-language libraries for immigrant readers, debate libraries for school students, and libraries compiled with club women in mind.

As the traveling library movement progressed, state library workers recognized the advantages of providing direct encouragement and advice to local communities. A library organizer (also called a "field worker" or "library visitor") could assess local conditions, establish traveling library stations, ensure that they were being properly managed, and arouse support for public libraries. In communities that had already established libraries, the organizer provided advice about facilities and equipment, helped with appeals to Andrew Carnegie for building grants, and assisted local—usually untrained—librarians with the organization of their work along modern lines. Ida Kidder, a library organizer in Washington and Oregon, could not see "how people are to be interested in books and libraries any other way."[19] Personal visits enabled library workers to see the scope and the possibilities within a region.

A pamphlet published in 1907 described the work of the library organizer, stating that it required "tireless energy, intimate acquaintance with conditions and people, an uncommon degree of inventive genius, and a thorough knowledge of the principles of advertising."

Requirements for a western library organizer included a few additional qualifications:

> A young woman who is not only a college graduate with library school training and experience . . . must be able to get along with Western people, ride and drive, as well as pack a horse, follow a trail, shoot straight, run an automobile, and be able to 'rough it' whenever necessary.[20]

During Cornelia Marvin's early years in Oregon, she made many personal visits to Oregon communities; however, California State Librarian James L. Gillis was among the first to employ a corps of women library organizers to canvas the state on behalf of traveling and public libraries.

The bulk of this organizing activity occurred during 1905 and 1906. When Mabel Prentiss (one of the California library organizers) resigned after three years, she looked with pride at the more than one hundred public libraries supported by taxation that she had assisted. Moreover, California organizers also ventured to Nevada where they provided assistance to the few library workers struggling to maintain libraries there.[21] Several other states employed organizers for brief periods, but most could not afford the heavy expense that accompanied this personalized form of library service in the rural West.

Gillis expected his organizers to be strong, courageous, confident, and outgoing. They traveled about the state by horseback, stage, team, train, and on foot, carrying the gospel of books to remote communities. Visits to mining towns where employees lived in company houses, and exposure to communities with "absolutely no chance for social gatherings," reinforced their belief in the power of libraries. Travel by train, accompanied primarily by salesmen, meant that they often arrived in towns during the early morning hours, had difficulty securing lodging, and sometimes were mistaken for "drummers" (traveling sales agents). When Bertha Kumli checked in at a Ukiah, California, hotel the clerk asked if one of her two bags was a sample case. "So you see," she wrote, "how I'm labeled."[22]

Gillis objected to one applicant on the basis of her youth, but gave her a trial appointment after a colleague countered: "Why should youth be a bar to a place that will require youth's energy and enthusiasm? . . . Has not the public speaking part of this position been

5.7. *Mabel Wilkinson on Joker, 1915.*
Courtesy Wyoming State Museum, Historical Research Section

overrated?'' Indeed, the young woman, once employed, mustered her courage and gave numerous speeches before clubs, congregations, and fraternal orders. She quickly discovered that "it is easy enough to speak before an audience if you have something to say."[23]

Although most of the organizing work occurred early in the century, some regions, because of geographic restraints, remained relatively untouched. In 1915, library organizer Mabel Wilkinson spent two weeks on horseback, taking the news about traveling libraries to settlers in Platte County, Wyoming. Her entire trip

had to be made on horseback, the journey covering about four hundred miles through very rough country, over poor roads and worse trails, with very few accommodations along the line.

Wilkinson quickly discovered that the countryside could change from day to day:

> Numerous claims are being filed on constantly, and while one may ride jauntily down a fairly good road from one hamlet to another, today, it is nothing to return on the morrow and find the road well fenced. Then there is nothing to do but scout around and keep going the general direction.

Wilkinson, as did other library visitors of this era, traveled alone. Because many remote areas could not be reached by rail or stage, she had to be an expert horsewoman. Wilkinson recounted the difficulty she experienced when trying to find a good saddle horse to transport her and a pack of books:

> Seven horses submitted were guaranteed to be absolutely gentle, tough, not afraid of anything and sound as a dollar. Two of them were so old that they could not have gone ten miles; one insisted on getting down on his knees every time there was a hill to be climbed; another stood straight on his hind legs and whirled around each time I mounted . . . ; another flatly refused to carry anything besides the rider; the sixth had a nasty habit of jumping violently to one side of the road without any reason or warning, and the seventh bucked his owner off before he got thru guaranteeing him! The eighth pony was a young bay, sound in wind and limb, extremely nervous and as quick as a cat . . . I mounted, fired a gun, put a pack on him, in fact took all the liberties with him that I could think of, and each time he 'made good,' so 'Joker' was chosen to be the library horse.

On her travels, Wilkinson "blazed away" at rattlesnakes with a Colt .38 revolver, encountered mad bulls, and discovered newly fenced claims blocking the paths she had only recently traversed. Main traveled roads suddenly went in three different directions or vanished all together. On one occasion she had to "ford an immense irrigation ditch several times, to the detriment of the appearance of all wearing apparel, both worn and packed." And to avoid the intense heat and

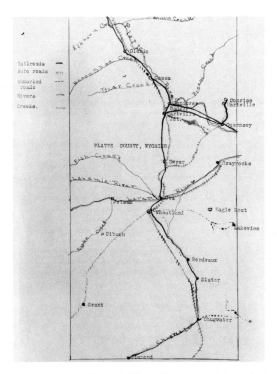

5.8. Map of Mabel Wilkinson's Platte County organizing trip, 1915.
Courtesy Wyoming State Museum, Historical Research Section

electrical storms that occurred late in the day, Wilkinson sometimes began her travels as early as two-thirty in the morning.

One day, Wilkinson found herself caught out in the sand hills as a storm approached. She "fairly strained her eyes seeking some form of shelter," and after galloping briskly for nearly an hour she "spied" a tiny claim shanty near a partially completed house:

> A young, simply clad Danish woman opened the door and
> in broken English bade me enter and bring the pony along!
> . . . I glanced inside the 'twelve by eighteen structure and
> beheld one room, the front end of which was occupied by
> the family of three, and the further end, partially curtained
> off, was occupied by four fairly good-sized horses crunching
> their hay.

5.9. Typical claim shanty, Chugwater Flats, Wyoming, 1915.
Courtesy Wyoming State Museum, Historical Research Section

The family invited Wilkinson to dine with them, and since no room remained for Joker at the horse-end of the shanty she "was handed a box of oats to hold on my lap so that 'Joker' could eat over my shoulder."

Wilkinson soon forgot the trials of travel after she encountered eager readers awaiting her visit and the library books she carried. She usually spoke to people assembled at the local post office, often a prospective site for the traveling library station. After giving her traveling library pitch in one community, Wilkinson discovered that she had "strayed" four miles beyond the boundaries of Platte County. People expressed great disappointment upon learning that they were not eligible for the service. She encountered farmers near Lakeview, "a tiny hamlet" in the heart of the Goshen Hole dry-farming district, who

> after hearing the explanation of the library scheme . . .
> jumped at the chance to obtain a traveling library, or in fact
> anything that resembled reading material, very much as a
> drowning person clutches a straw.

5.10. Hartville, Wyoming, 1915.
Courtesy Wyoming State Museum, Historical Research Section

Wilkinson also delivered her messages in churches, and ministers often expressed eagerness to have collections of books in their communities. The pastor of the Presbyterian church in Sunrise, a town where everything appeared to be "owned by the Colorado Fuel and Iron Co.," arranged for Wilkinson to "call on each family, including the Greek and Italian workingmen." She found them "overjoyed at the prospect of getting something to read," and before she departed she had persuaded the manager of the Colorado Fuel and Iron Company to "furnish a room with three reading tables, chairs, book cases, heat and lights."

In some communities, however, Wilkinson had to overcome doubts about the traveling library plan. The postmistress in Bordeau, "flatly refused to have anything to do with the traveling library proposition. She was suspicious of anything supposed to be free." After some casual conversation, in which Wilkinson mentioned that she had attended some "hard-shell" Baptist meetings, the woman began to "look with favor on the proposition. Only one community—Hartville Junction—rejected the library proposition unconditionally."[24]

The strenuous work of promoting public libraries in western communities appealed to library school graduates afire with "library spirit." Basking in the glow of a successful library campaign, California organizer Mabel Prentiss confided to State Librarian James Gillis:

They think the State Library should receive a vote of thanks
for sending me down here . . . [they] call it leading them
out of darkness . . . I really wish I could tell you how
pleased I am with the result of twenty-four hours work.

Prentiss thrived on the work that included more successes than fail-
ures, concluding: "I always did love to bring order out of chaos." In
addition to the actual work of organizing library campaigns, these
women relished the adventure inherent in their travels about the state.
Prentiss and Kumli good-naturedly peppered their correspondence
with humorous references to adverse conditions: "I thought of tele-
graphing you for wading boots and a slicker and towards night decided
to ask also for a boat."[25]

One of the organizer's first activities, in a town that had no previously existing library, was to enlist the support of respected community
leaders—ministers, newspaper editors, elected officials. They pro-
ceeded aggressively, often calling upon a dozen or more people each
day. Organizers recognized the necessity of recruiting men to the
cause, but openly acknowledged that men "seldom work for such a
project as the women do." As a result, they often collaborated with
wives in the cause. When the city clerk in one town spoke disparagingly
about the public library campaign, the library organizer visited him in
his wife's presence and the two "did not let him express himself—just
took it for granted that *he* was heartily in favor." It became essential to
win the support of newspaper editors, who could give visibility to the
library movement. Although the editor of the Auburn, California, *Her-
ald* was "conservative," his wife persuaded him to give up "*three* inches
of space headed 'Public Library.'" Kumli attributed her success to the
fact that "*She liked me.*"[26]

One of the California organizers had planned to call upon a saloon man at his place of work, but found herself hiking "over hills and
dales out in the country to see him" at his residence because his
establishment had no back door. It was inconceivable, she wrote, for
her to be seen entering such an establishment. In general, organizers
believed that the men of the community were "slightly indifferent,"
but nonetheless "willing to be interested and only too glad to be
relieved from all responsibility" for the development of a library.[27]

After securing the endorsement of civic leaders, organizers typically enlisted a few key people to circulate petitions in support of

establishing a tax-supported public library. They then submitted the signed petitions to town or city councils for action. The key to success, organizers believed, lay in getting "people to take hold of the petitions who will not antagonize [the public]." Occasionally local library enthusiasts hindered the cause more than they advanced it. One of the California organizers, for example, expressed dismay after she met an ardent supporter who she described as "what is commonly called a 'crank' . . . He *has* brains, a kindly heart, but he *is* peculiar and while he was talking my heart sank."[28]

As they took a community's political and social pulse, organizers learned much about local politics. The Women's Christian Temperance Union, for example, withdrew support of the library proposal in one community because the organizer supported the Improvement Club's plans to hold card parties and dances in order to raise money for the library. And the women's club in Martinez, California, gave a number of reasons for their reluctance to turn their club library over to the community, among them: It might get into politics, a saloon might locate on the same block, the town trustees might cut its income, and the books would wear out sooner. Such conditions frustrated library workers and inevitably diminished some of their commitment to the democratic process. After struggling with the warring residents of one community, Mabel Prentiss declared that residents needed a strong measure of paternal care: "Starting a library here is like trying to drive a blind horse. They are one and the same willing, scared, and stupid."[29]

Before the library question came to a vote, library organizers attempted to alleviate concerns and resolve objections by holding a series of public meetings. Naturally, such meetings could not conflict with other important community events, for example, a traveling minstrel show or a revival. Bertha Kumli quickly discovered that evening meetings were unsuccessful in Auburn, California, because people lived "on hills and down valleys" and had "to carry lanterns with 'em when they go visiting nights."[30] In lieu of weekday meetings, organizers sometimes accepted invitations from ministers and liberal priests to appear in the pulpit on Sunday mornings. In such instances, they usually faced sympathetic audiences.

Most religious leaders supported the public library idea. A library organizer in Utah described the Church of Jesus Christ of Latter-day Saints as "a great aid to promoting library work" because it was interested in social betterment, and she spent many Sundays attending and speaking at services. Roman Catholic priests, however, sometimes expressed reservations because they feared that parishioners would begin reading secular materials. On at least one occasion, organizer Bertha Kumli managed to win the support of a German Catholic priest by striking up a conversation in his native tongue: "You see," she said, "it's worth while to be Dutch occasionally."[31]

Opposition to public libraries developed for a variety of other reasons. Town councils often equated a library with a building, and consequently objected on the basis of inadequate funding for construction. Many communities suffered from bonded indebtedness for waterworks, courthouses, and streets. This made it difficult to win over leading citizens, especially when they shouldered heavy tax assessments. Mabel Prentiss encountered an unsympathetic hotel owner, the heaviest taxpayer in Monterey, who discouraged her campaign: "Last year's bills are some of them still unpaid . . . there is not enough money to run the town as it is now."[32]

Some residents equated the phrase "public library" with "Carnegie Library." In fact, one organizer reported that she had encountered a civic leader who wanted a Carnegie library—"no *Public Library* for him!" For some communities a Carnegie Library building represented a stage of progress, and they focused on the physical building while overlooking the importance of adequate books and trained librarians. Bertha Kumli reported that the "dear people" of Ukiah, California, wanted a Carnegie building "more than a collection of books," a fact that she had to "work against." Later, bitterness surfaced when she described a club woman who wanted "a Carnegie library or nothing at all—wouldn't raise a finger if the 'library' meant a dingy dark room."[33]

In other communities, lack of support for libraries was attributed to external factors, such as the railroad and tax structures. The Superintendent of Public Instruction in Idaho City, Idaho, attributed the lack of support for libraries there to the fact that the county was "not blessed with railroads" and had very few saloons, which meant little revenue from license money, while in Rocklin, California, residents hesitated to tax themselves for a library because they feared that the railroad shops would move and leave men unemployed.[34]

Organizers also visited communities where too many groups had already circulated petitions to build churches and schools. Opponents of libraries often argued that those who wanted to read could buy books. Several residents of Blackfoot, Idaho, for example, objected to taxing "all the people for the benefit of a very few where the library may be situated." When organizers convinced influential citizens to support the library cause, however, more general support usually followed. Mabel Prentiss reported that after she had won "*the* man of the Council . . . and could quote him, the others began to thaw."[35]

Residents in some communities hesitated to support the public library movement because earlier efforts to maintain library associations or reading rooms had failed, or because they previously had fallen prey to fraudulent traveling library companies. Even legitimate concerns focused more on sales than on the maintenance of the collections they distributed. The head of the Parmalee Traveling Library Company boasted in 1895 that "the clever solicitor can, on the average, place five . . . per month."[36] Because these books tended to stagnate after solicitors departed, citizens became convinced that a new library would share a similar fate.

The library organizers expressed concern about being perceived as paternalistic, but nonetheless considered it essential in many areas. After being confronted with numerous excuses, Mabel Prentiss became frustrated with residents of Salinas, California, and the "hopeless way in which everyone has said 'Oh, we want a library, but we can't have one because' . . ." She also found the situation in Gilroy "a bit hard to handle . . . because they already knew their own minds well enough to resent any paternalism." Her counterpart, Bertha Kumli, believed the paternalistic approach to be the only way that some communities could be persuaded to do what was, in her mind, for their best interest. Referring to the communities she visited as her "library children," Kumli did not want to "let the poor orphans struggle on by themselves." Their exposure to small western communities also awakened these library organizers to the fact that western libraries would have to be developed along more simple lines than the eastern urban exemplars depicted in much of the professional literature.[37]

After educating community residents about the library proposition, organizers next took the matter to the town council for a vote. There, where citizens with some of the heaviest tax burdens assembled, the organizer had to be her most persuasive. Mabel Prentiss encountered a powerful opponent at the Lincoln, California, council meeting:

He is nearly seventy-five, a very profane old man,
uneducated and absolutely impossible to reason with. He
flatly told me he didn't care what the law was, that he had
opposed a library and should continue to.

Prentiss refused to quarrel with him, instead addressing her remarks to
the remaining council members. She met with success, and

after a little the other members began to laugh at him and
side with me. . . . Then the role was called, and one by one
they voted aye until Mr. Gray's name was called. You could
have heard a pin drop, and when he fairly snorted 'Aye' . . .
all the audience cheered.[38]

The organizers' work did not end after the library proposition
passed the town council. State library organizers also provided instruction to local librarians in the technical aspects of library work—how to
catalog according to the Dewey Decimal system, where to place orders,
what supplies to use—and she attempted to inculcate them with the
true library spirit. All too often, however, they encountered librarians
and trustees who viewed libraries as warehouses for books rather than
dynamic cultural agencies. When Bertha Kumli visited the library in
Newcastle, she found "about 300 books nicely placed away in a nice
closet locked up in the hall of their building," where no one would
ever find it. Her assessment of Eureka, California, was: "Trustees fos-
sils. Librarian ditto."[39]

Local librarians generally gave library organizers a warm welcome.
Occasionally, however, they awaited the organizer's visit with nervous
anticipation, believing that they were being inspected by an expert or
specialist. No matter how pleasant their personalities and good their
intentions, local librarians frequently lacked a broader vision of the
work and a wide knowledge of books. Moreover, they could become
too easily satisfied with their meager results. Yet one organizer could
not help but be sympathetic when she encountered a widowed local
librarian who paid another woman twelve dollars of her twenty-five
dollar monthly salary to care for her two children while she worked.[40]

In communities where the librarian's position stood vacant, residents sometimes appeared distrustful because they suspected that the
organizer might favor one candidate or another:

They more than half suspected me to be working for one candidate or the other, and [I] found out for a fact that the reason I found so few at home was that they were being run to death by friends of first one and then the other.[41]

Public library trustees often preferred to put "local girls" in charge of the books because "local salaries would hardly pay car-fare for a competent worker" who would have to travel "over-whelming distances from library centres [sic]."[42] Few possessed the appropriate qualifications, but many coveted the job. When local residents vied for the position of librarian, organizers sometimes had to serve as mediators. Candidates frequently included poor women, widows anxious to earn a living for themselves and their children, or elderly men. Kumli found one seventy-five-year-old man in charge of a local library, "a cripple— uses both a cane and a crutch, and tho' he's been in [office] for three months can't charge a book yet." And when communities decided to hire "foreign" professionals, the displaced amateur librarians expressed resentment when they were demoted to the position of assistant: "I am to supply the brains for $45 per month while she takes the honors and the salary."[43]

Nonetheless, organizers often felt as though they had become part of the various communities they assisted. After spending two days in Gilroy, Mabel Prentiss concluded: "I felt as though I were leaving friends of long standing." And although the conditions under which Bertha Kumli labored had been difficult— including insufficient help and limited supplies ("I'd give all three of my future husbands and my smile for a few ordinary supplies")—she thrived on the challenge of making books available to readers in California's gold country:

> I can just see all of you enjoying the comforts of home . . .
> and I tramping about with draggled skirts interviewing
> folks—but I'm having lots of fun, and you aren't.[44]

~ six ~

Creating the Library Habit

When public library trustees decided to appoint a professionally trained librarian, they usually turned to state librarians, state library commission workers, and library school directors for the names of suitable candidates. In carefully worded, detailed letters they described their community, the residents, the library's condition, and the salary they expected to offer. Trustees also specified the traits that they thought a successful librarian needed to possess—physical endurance, intellectual ability, a pleasant personality, and an ability to adapt to western life. In other words, they wanted to import a leader.

Trustees expressed a preference for western-born librarians, or those who had some familiarity with the region, but few with training were available. Awareness of conditions and limitations in new communities and institutions would lessen, trustees believed, the librarian's frustration. Cornelia Marvin's belief that western women would adapt more easily to pioneer conditions led her to agitate for the establishment of a western library school. She found it "quite crushing to have them [eastern and midwestern women] disillusioned through their first experience."[1] Her correspondence includes numerous letters documenting the difficulty that western women had "in getting admitted to any first class institution [library school]." Moreover, they resented having "to cross a continent to obtain the preparation needed."[2]

Mary Frances Isom, librarian of the Library Association of Portland, found herself inundated with people she considered unqualified to enter her public library training class. Isom expected applicants to possess a high school diploma, some college education, and a broad knowledge of history and literature. Many, she surmised, viewed the position of librarian as a sinecure. Prior to giving an entrance examination in 1905—which included questions about current events, literary works, historical events, and several passages of foreign language to be translated—Isom confided: "I am in perfect despair over my applicants for tomorrow. I have few under eighty-five. . . . Most of them have husbands, and in some cases whole families wish to take the examination and join us in body."[3]

Cornelia Marvin worked with Isom to transform the latter's public library training class into the West's first year-long library school. Their plans, however, depended upon Andrew Carnegie's benevolence. In 1911 Isom informed Marvin that she had written the letter "to Mr. Bertram [Carnegie's Executive Secretary] that we planned and it is almost time for me to hear from him. I am quite excited over it." Two years later, however, plans for the school had not materialized and Isom began to sound discouraged: "Do you think we ever shall get a library school? I hear nothing more from Mr. Carnegie and I don't dare write." By the end of the year she accepted the fact that Carnegie would not look favorably on the proposal. She had learned from an eastern colleague that "Mr. Carnegie seems to be irritated whenever the Portland school was mentioned and he advised us to say nothing more for sometime."[4]

State librarian J. L. Gillis recognized an even greater need to establish a school in California. In 1909, legislators, however, nixed his plan to open a library school at the state library. Gillis nonetheless moved ahead with plans for an apprentice-style training class which he opened in January 1914. Offered until 1918, each class consisted of up to ten students who worked for three to six months under his supervision in the state library. The fall before the class began he justified his actions to a skeptical Marvin:

> The best of the people in California are employed and the demand here is greater than we can fill. For that reason we are establishing a library school in the State Library . . . in an attempt to try and secure qualified assistants for our work.

Gillis further assured Marvin that he had "waited a long time for the Universities and for others to take up this work, but nothing has been done."[5]

Familiarity with the region could be an asset, but library trustees also recognized that a socially adept librarian could promote the library cause more effectively than could a timid, albeit technically capable, woman. The board of the public library in Pendleton, Oregon, for example, specified that their librarian should be "a good 'mixer' . . . something of a society girl . . . who dances and plays cards." Residents there, they stressed, would not tolerate a librarian who appeared to be intellectually superior. A New Mexico community sought "a *live* librarian, one who . . . can meet the people cordially, and one who has enough initiative to seize the opportunity to make the library helpful and popular."[6] Public library trustees—especially those in small communities—seldom sought male librarians, believing them to be more expensive and less likely to remain for an extended period.

While religious affiliations were not "the test of admission to the position," some employers refused to make appointments without knowing a candidate's faith. A few even specified the denomination that would be most acceptable to a particular community. Roman Catholic librarians experienced the greatest discrimination, probably because of their minority status in many western communities and because Protestants feared that they would proselytize. An eastern library school director felt "obliged" to inform a potential employer that an applicant was Roman Catholic, but assured her that although the student had previously "permitted her strong religious prejudices to color her library work," experience had taught her "the place that her religion must occupy in her life and work."[7] One Wyoming branch librarian found herself serving a "half Mormon and half Gentile" county seat. The library movement succeeded, however, because the young librarian, "herself a Mormon, was much interested in the world and anxious to bring it to her town."[8]

A library board's decision to employ a graduate librarian did not guarantee that the community, or even all of the board members, supported and understood the need for her appointment. After reporting to work, one western librarian learned that the board had voted four to three in her favor. Seeing her in action, however, persuaded "the most bitter opponents," who confided to her that they could "see now that an untrained person couldn't have done what I have done."[9] Many other librarians encountered similar situations, and recognized the necessity of developing a larger appreciation for the library and their work.

Trustees sometimes hinted to their librarian that the amount of her salary depended on her ability to generate support for the library. Ritzville, Washington, trustees urged their librarian to hold entertainments that would stimulate interest in the library and raise money. They promised that, if she succeeded, they "might be able to increase the salary."[10] Other communities, recognizing that they could not afford to pay what a professional librarian required, suggested alternative ways of making ends meet. Sometimes board members proposed that a prospective librarian supplement her salary by teaching kindergarten or working as a stenographer when the library was closed.

Board members in a number of communities did not fully comprehend the nature and extent of a professional librarian's responsibilities. The board in Mill Valley, California, delegated one of its members to ask the state librarian to

> kindly tell us what are the duties of the librarian? Is she
> supposed to see to having books rebound. . . . There is
> constantly a question as to 'Is this my business or is it not?'

Another board had never inquired of the local government how much money the library could expect from city appropriations, and board members informed the librarian that she had overstepped her bounds when she suggested that they investigate. Such situations reinforced to these librarians the importance of giving trustees a better understanding of modern library work. When librarians complained about their boards, library school directors reminded them of their "grand" opportunity to convert "faddists" into "real" trustees with a broader view of the work.[11]

Youthful, inexperienced librarians, however, often felt intimidated by boards of trustees composed of prominent citizens. Library boards could be all-male or mixed, but few were all-female. The mayor usually appointed library trustees, subject to approval by the city or town council, but occasionally they were chosen by popular election. Some librarians found it easier to work with male trustees, convinced that men, as civic leaders, could push things through. Others preferred to work with women, believing that they possessed a deeper interest in the library. A few, however, described women trustees as possessive, fussy, jealous, and reluctant to give up control.

Occasionally, librarians wrote about the collegial relationships they enjoyed with board members. Ida Kidder delighted in the composition of the Tacoma, Washington, board, that consisted of "educated and cultured" people—a superintendent of schools, an Episcopal Bishop, a retired capitalist, a leading club woman, and the wife of judge. And a Deer Lodge, Montana, librarian praised her board, "typical western men," who gave her anything she requested, provided that she offered them a good reason and that funds were available.[12]

Others, however, found themselves working under the direction of uninformed, miserly men and women who refused to give their librarian any authority. An Oregon librarian expressed dismay upon learning that she was not permitted to select books. Instead, a board member carried out this activity, and she described his choices as "far from useful." Another librarian described the board of a California community as "the most helpless individuals" she had ever met. Prior to her arrival in November:

> They ordered about 150 books—and have had them on
> hand since last March and were waiting for aid. . . . The
> books they did get are a lot of miserably cheap reprints.
> About the only other thing they did do was to have an
> immense sign 'Public Library' painted and placed it in front
> of a house where there wasn't a public library.[13]

The precedent for trustees selecting books stemmed from the time when amateur librarians managed local collections. With the arrival of professionally trained women, boards gradually relinquished this responsibility, but selections usually remained subject to the board's approval.

Like the academic librarians, newly appointed public librarians often inherited libraries in much need of organization. Mayme Batterson reported to the faculty of the Illinois Library School soon after her arrival in Pendleton, Oregon, in 1909:

> I have been so very busy ever since I arrived, which together
> with a very severe cold, due to change of climate and a cold
> library room the first two days, accounts for the delay.

6.1. Raton, New Mexico, Public Library, ca. 1912.
Courtesy Arthur Johnson Memorial Library

Even though Batterson, illustrative of many western librarians, encountered "perplexing problems" that "one would not meet in a larger library or in a town where the library had been in existence for awhile," she thrived on the challenges confronting her and believed that she had found "just the work for me, for I love it more all the time."[14]

Disheveled piles of worn books housed in one or two unheated rooms, and readers expecting immediate progress, greeted some of the librarians, while a few began work in newly constructed Carnegie libraries. The construction of a library building often led to the appointment of the community's first trained librarian, but in other instances communities appointed graduate librarians expecting them to assist with appeals to Andrew Carnegie for a building grant.

That library schools of this era emphasized the value of organization and efficiency is evident in the librarians' earliest activities. Public librarians, like their counterparts in academic libraries, made cataloging and classification two of their early priorities. Setting to work, often alone or assisted by a school girl or a few volunteers from local women's clubs, graduate librarians often became overwhelmed by the monumental task of bringing order to chaos. Several women reported

6.2. Librarian Myrtle Cole and an assistant in the Raton, New Mexico, Public Library.
Courtesy Arthur Johnson Memorial Library

spending their evenings and weekends in the library–cataloging, classifying, and establishing order on the shelves. A Colorado librarian described her daily existence, which included "an infinite amount of detail work," mending, desk work, reference work, work with school children and the clubs. Her only assistants included a school girl who gave her a few hours daily in return for the training, and a young boy who considered his work done after he had "built a fire in the furnace and swept the middle of the floor."[15]

Lacking many of the necessary tools, recent graduates implored library school faculty to send advice about the cataloging of certain titles. In addition to the sought-after advice, directors gave them gentle admonitions, reminding them that it was more important for them to circulate in their communities than it was to have each book in perfect order. Viewing the technical work as merely a means to an end, public librarians, again like academic librarians, modified cataloging and classification rules by eliminating all useless details except those necessary "for the bringing of a book and reader together."[16]

6.3. "Typical Beginnings," 1915.
Courtesy Wyoming State Museum, Historical Research Section

The newly arrived librarians found existing collections to be of varying quality. Established largely through donations, library holdings typically included the remnants of earlier libraries and worn, outdated, dull, or uninteresting titles discarded from private libraries. Early in its history, for example, the Public Library of Las Vegas, New Mexico, had filled its shelves with ten sacks of government publication donated by a congressional delegate. Not being high circulation items, these documents collected dust while the public clamored for more interesting titles.

Librarians recognized the necessity of discarding worn and outdated titles so they would not obscure works of greater interest. Nonetheless, they hesitated to commence weeding projects because they did not wish to offend the members of the community who had donated books for the library cause. Moreover, many communities took great pride in the size of their library collections, associating quality with quantity. Such factors did not deter one western librarian, however, who when confronted with the "sadness" of a collection consisting of 2,000 donations, called upon her "spare mites of courage" and reduced it to 350 volumes.[17] Librarians also devoted many hours to mending books in the absence of local binderies. Sending books East for repair proved to be too costly and time-consuming.

Strained budgets prohibited the librarians from purchasing such basic supplies as Library of Congress cards and typewriters, and when they placed orders for paste, labels, and shelving from Eastern supply companies they experienced lengthy delays. A Hoquiam, Washington, librarian expected to "be confronted any moment by a U.S. Marshall" because she had vented her anger by penning irate epistles to the Library Bureau (a library supply company) in Chicago. Others contracted to have such items as shelving and book trucks constructed locally but, in the case of the latter, still had to send East for the wheels.[18]

After establishing a semblance of order, public librarians turned their attention and energies to extending the library's influence throughout the community. Indeed, many early-twentieth-century librarians considered this to be one of the most important, and most appealing, aspects of their work. An Oregon librarian, recalling her motivation for entering the profession, recalled: "I took up the work . . . because of its opportunity for social service."[19] Western librarians promoted libraries through library columns in the local paper, notices in church bulletins, and by persuading newspaper editors to write editorials endorsing public library work. They also gave numerous talks to a variety of civic and social organizations. Little wonder that trustees regarded an outgoing personality as a prerequisite for library work.

Like many educators of this era, librarians believed access to books would help children "progress to the ideal completeness that the creator intended for them."[20] Although public libraries had not catered to children during much of the nineteenth century, beginning in the 1890s librarians lowered age limits, created children's rooms or corners, appointed children's librarians, and sent collections of books to city playgrounds. Unfortunately, few western libraries had many books appropriate for young readers. A library organizer in Wyoming recalled one child "who wandered forlornly through the stacks for an hour, patiently hunting for . . . the few juvenile books distributed among the common shelves."[21]

Few early western librarians possessed special training in children's work, but they nonetheless devoted a great deal of energy to this aspect of their work. Librarians in large public libraries initiated a number of special programs for children. The Los Angeles Public Library sent collections of books to playgrounds as early as 1906. One of Mary Frances Isom's early actions included the establishment of a children's

6.4. Wheatland's First Story Hour, 1915.
Courtesy Wyoming State Museum, Historical Research Section

library league at the Public Library of Portland: "We are very new and crude out here, and pinched with poverty, but hope springs eternal." She aimed to instill the library habit in every child who lived within walking distance of a public library, a branch library, or a deposit station. Isom also instituted weekly "Oregon stories" in which pioneers came to the library and shared their early Oregon experiences with children. Librarians followed up these talks by offering related books and pictures, making the program fill a dual purpose—instilling in children a knowledge of state history, and advertising the library.[22]

Isom, firmly convinced that libraries could empower children by educating them for a lifetime, expressed grave concern for the ones who did not use them. Schools taught children how to read, but Isom regarded this was "a curse instead of a blessing" because they did not teach children what to read. She cited the case of one neighborhood boy, whose exposure to "lurid plays" at neighboring nickelodeons had led him to steal money from his employer and buy pistols for himself and his friends. Her conviction that the library must intervene led to the appointment, in 1902, of a librarian whose sole responsibility was to work with children. Isom encouraged this children's librarian "to work it up to a proper basis . . . particularly in gaining the confidence of the teachers and aiding the schools."[23] In an attempt to reach children, she prepared enticing displays, developed recommended lists of books, began story hours, and visited playgrounds and boys clubs.

Work with rural communities posed a variety of challenges. There librarians began by assessing existing efforts to serve young readers. Ida Kidder visited one Oregon library that contained a "few hit or miss (mostly miss) children's books" under the supervision of "a young man studying law, who charges a book when a child screws up his courage to ask that favor." In Platte County, Wyoming, Mabel Wilkinson discovered an energetic local woman who offered a story hour, but failed to recognize "the importance of the story hour leading to *books which the children can get*."[24]

School district libraries often proved to be an effective means of providing rural library service in lieu of tax-supported public libraries. Teachers typically served as librarians in their spare hours, and graduate librarians feared that teachers, working alone, would make unwise book selections. Moreover, they recognized that selection decisions often rested with members of the school board. Therefore, graduate librarians in public libraries developed several ways to intervene. These included classroom visits, the preparation of buying lists for teachers and school boards, and provision of carefully selected traveling libraries. Librarians also appeared on the programs of teachers' and farmers' institutes, where they delivered lectures about "the possibilities for self-improvement within their reach."[25]

Books in school district libraries easily became scattered because teachers changed constantly and schoolhouses were closed for long periods during the summer. When Linda Clatworthy surveyed Colorado's school libraries in 1915, she discovered that the Cripple Creek schools had ten thousand school library books located in fourteen school buildings, and teachers had no mechanism for exchange or the elimination of unnecessary duplication. Thus, a sizeable collection did not necessarily signify quality.

In sparsely populated areas, for example, children did not even have access to traveling library collections. In 1909 the New Mexico Territorial Board of Education commissioned Julia Brown Asplund to collect statistics on school libraries. Asplund, a graduate of the Drexel

Institute Library School, had arrived in New Mexico six years earlier. Her investigation revealed five counties with no school libraries, and a number of other counties where only the town schools had library service. Asplund recommended that a system of traveling libraries be established to aid the country teachers who labored under extreme poverty, but geography prevailed and such a system did not develop for many years. Even as late as 1946 when Asplund conducted another study, more than half of New Mexico's population remained unserved.[26]

Western librarians, like their counterparts in the East, made children's work a priority, but they also devoted substantial energy to reaching adult nonreaders. Many had a ready-made adult clientele consisting of club women, teachers, business men, civic leaders, and aspiring clerks. Recognizing that many citizens regarded the library as a haven for women and children, a number of librarians—especially those in larger communities—established separate reading rooms for men. Typically housed in the basement, such rooms occasionally permitted smoking. According to Raymond Held, men could smoke in the public libraries of Alameda and Fresno, California.[27] Librarians also developed collections of books—for example, scientific and technical works—intended to interest male readers.

After organizing her library, Mayme Batterson considered her "greatest problem" to be that of how to interest people, especially the ones "who have no books in their own homes and who, therefore, need the library." In addition to listing new acquisitions in the local newspaper, Batterson traveled from door to door distributing leaflets and extending personal invitations to visit the library. She held a series of library evenings, specifically targeting the community's working-class residents: "We typed neat little invitations on 'P' slips using the carbon, and I took them around to all the homes in that district, giving a personal invitation when I had the chance."[28] Once in her library, visitors found attractive bulletin boards, typewritten lists of books, and displays of books from each class on the tables.

The racially and culturally homogeneous western librarians believed that they were advancing western society to a higher plane by perpetuating their own cherished Euro-American literature and traditions. To that end, they developed playground libraries for racial and ethnic minorities in Los Angeles, circulated books to an Indian school in Oregon, and provided foreign-language materials to immigrants in

Seattle. After attracting diverse groups to the library with popular, high-interest materials, they then attempted to redirect their interest to items belonging to the prevailing cultural canon.

Librarians carried boxes containing books in both English and foreign languages to communities with large immigrant populations. The concept of free library service was unheard of in many of their native countries. Librarians expressed feelings of satisfaction when they observed "school children showing their parents where to find books in the mother tongue." After the priest announced to the parishioners of a Polish settlement in Portland that Polish books could be obtained at a branch library, Mary Frances Isom expressed delight because "every day sees a new Polish member, man or woman." Because the immigrant children read English books, Isom knew that it would not be long before the parents would be more fully Americanized. Indeed, librarians regarded most immigrants as "anxious to become Americanized."[29]

Librarians provided books in Spanish and other European languages, but their silence concerning Asian-language materials suggests either that it was not possible to obtain such works or that they were unfamiliar with eastern languages and literature and thus avoided the topic. A librarian in Los Angeles, delighted in her encounters with "Spaniards, Mexicans, Syrians and all kinds of white and black folk," noted that access to library books "helped them wonderfully in learning English." The children, she noted, read English books. And in Oregon, Cornelia Marvin devoted a great deal of energy to improving Native American children's access to books. On a visit to the "Indian School at Chemawa," she was distressed to discover that it was "entirely without books for young children."[30] Rather than criticize, Marvin developed a plan of cooperation with the Bureau of Indian Affairs.

Early-twentieth-century librarians accepted as one of their primary missions the responsibility "to guard against worthless fiction." Maintaining a conservative, even elitist stance, they delighted in seeing "these books which we all love and cherish and consider part of our lawful inheritance" reach people for the first time. Many of the collections graduate librarians inherited—consisting as they did of gifts and discards, included titles the librarians considered inappropriate for young readers. Mary Frances Isom removed several titles from the children's collection at the Public Library of Portland, among them the works of Horatio Alger and Oliver Optic. Others discarded the

"Elsie" books, describing them as "too sentimental and trashy," and Cornelia Marvin removed "Rab and his friends" from the recommended list of books for schools because she considered the description of an operation for cancer "entirely unfit for them."[31]

In an effort to guide local librarians in their selection of books, state library commission workers issued buying lists that included such endorsed authors and titles as Arthur Colon Doyle's *Hound of the Baskervilles*, Bret Harte's *Openings in the Old Trail*, and Owen Wister's *The Virginian*. Other popular titles included Mark Twain's *Roughing It* and *Innocents Abroad*, Booker T. Washington's *Up From Slavery*, and *Pride and Prejudice*, *Little Dorritt*, and *Ben-Hur*. For children, they recommended Robert Louis Stevenson's *A Child's Garden of Verses* and Howard Pyle's *Some Merry Adventures of Robin-Hood*. Children also favored Kipling's *Jungle Book* and the works of Louisa May Alcott.[32]

While librarians wanted to foster interest in reading, they also wanted to discourage the reading of too much fiction. A Pendleton, Oregon, librarian tried to stimulate interest in higher-quality books by continually changing a display near the circulation desk, labeled "Books Worth Reading." She reported success with this venture, observing that readers, after seeing the books, often took one of them instead of a novel. Isom encouraged her branch librarians to supervise readers' choices, and librarians in Colorado and Oregon, finding it difficult to stem the public's growing interest in fiction, initiated a plan of charging ten cents per volume for new fiction until it was six months old.[33]

Cornelia Marvin recognized the difficulty of steering rural Oregonians away from fiction. In the country, she wrote, fiction took "the place of many of the social institutions of the city—theatres, moving-picture shows, etc., frequently of churches and church life." Nonetheless, during World War I she returned to her original insistence on high-quality literature, adopting "No new fiction until after the war" as the state library slogan. While most librarians had little success in discouraging the public's appetite for fiction, one observed that as long as Billy Sunday was holding revivals in her community, requests for novels declined. Nonetheless, she fully expected "the back sliders" to return after his departure.[34]

As funds for traveling libraries and library organizers lessened, continuing concern for rural readers prompted librarians to develop a more permanent form of rural library service—the county library. California had initiated a "library without walls" in 1903 as an extension of the state library. This traveling library system, modeled on Dewey's New York State example, reached areas unserved by municipal libraries. California presented special challenges to this model, however, with several counties larger than eastern states, and counties where many languages and cultures coexisted. And even though populated by educated people, many California communities remained unable to provide adequate financial support for public libraries.

State Librarian James L. Gillis soon recognized the desirability of making the county, instead of the state, the distribution center for library materials for California's rapidly growing rural population. Gillis, state librarian from 1899 until his death in 1917, believed that "the county people and the schools are the ones most interested and the ones who are demanding that they have an even chance for library privileges with those living in the city." He also was convinced that the term "county library" would have greater appeal to people who associated the term "public library" with "city library."

The 1909 County Free Library Law represented a significant first step for Gillis, and with the appointment of educator Harriet G. Eddy as the first "official" county library organizer, the state library and public education became allies. Gillis soon recognized the shortcomings of the 1909 law, and began working for a revised law designed to secure results. It passed the legislature in 1911.[35]

California's county libraries experienced immediate success, perhaps because Gillis discontinued the state's traveling library service and forced readers to turn to their local units. While trained librarians supervised the work from the county seat—selecting materials, preparing them for circulation, and establishing reading rooms and deposit stations throughout the county—the reading rooms and deposit stations could be staffed by volunteers or untrained assistants. This system brought the library closer to people who lived far from the city's center and, to some extent, resembled the branch library system prevalent in urban communities of the eastern United States. As a result, communities that could not afford to establish a public library or employ a trained librarian could have library services comparable to their urban counterparts.

With the establishment of county libraries came a means to standardize and coordinate school library collections. School boards turned their book budgets over to county librarians who in turn

Creating the Library Habit ～ 117

bought books more economically and efficiently. Books from a consolidated collection then could be circulated on request to individual schools, operating much like the state traveling libraries had. County librarians derived a great deal of satisfaction from preparing these shipments of books—Greek myths, stories of famous prisons and prisoners, biographies—for the country schools: "You are so certain of the joy you are giving the children."[36]

Thus, librarians throughout the country came to view California as a model in what they regarded as "the next great phase of library development." Librarians in states where library work developed at a slower pace envied California's success in reaching rural readers:

> On the rockbound coast, in the desert, in the mountains
> you see the California County library sign. Books are
> transported by mule, by airplane and every other
> conceivable method.[37]

County library work represented yet another outlet for librarians drawn to librarianship because of its potential for educational service and missionary work. Although she had a secure position in New Jersey, Sarah Askew considered a move to Oregon in 1913 because there a librarian could "hold a county as you never could a state and the work in building it up would be fascinating." Della Northey, appointed librarian in Hood River, Oregon, in 1912, found it "necessary to come way out here in order to get the kind of work" she wanted, work where she could "see results from day to day."[38]

Believing in the potential of the county library to reach a previously unserved population, librarians approached their work with a renewed zeal. Northey described her efforts to reach county readers:

> I am very enthusiastic over the work and its possibilities. . . .
> The other night I visited a little community up in the
> mountains taking with me a box of books intending to give
> a little book talk and leave them if they cared to have them.
> Imagine my disappointment when I found that a patent
> medicine show had come to the place and that all the
> people were assembled there. . . . And so the librarian of
> Hood River County Library was announced between the acts

at the picture show, she gave her little book talk and left her books.[39]

Anne Hadden displayed a similar spirit in Monterey County, California, when she traveled with a Spanish guide and, "in eleven days, by train seventy miles, about sixty by stage, thirty or more on horseback and seventy miles on foot," established two branches of the county library and visited a third.[40] In Chouteau County, Montana, the librarian attempted to "get hold of" the country people through a system of twenty branches. Her counterpart in Medford, Oregon, made plans to extend service to 150 country schools and to maintain a mail-order service for county residents unserved by branch libraries or deposit stations.[41]

At an early stage of development, California state librarian James L. Gillis had recognized the importance of involving the public school system in the county library movement. Schools represented effective distribution centers, and school-library cooperation also yielded economic benefits for both. In an outline of the plan, a county library worker explained:

> Any district may turn over its library funds to the county
> librarian, who thus becomes a co-operative purchaser,
> getting at wholesale where the trustees had to buy at retail,
> avoiding duplication where much now exists, and circulating
> the books all around the county where now they lie idle so
> long in one district.[42]

County library workers, like the traveling library workers who preceded them, cited numerous examples of satisfied readers. They observed men and boys—forced to relinquish school days for employment—now eager to make considerable use of scientific and mechanical books. Everett R. Perry, librarian for Imperial County and the Los Angeles Public Library, praised county work, reaching as it did "a family who live out forty miles on the desert claim" who "could never have the privilege of having books were it not for the County Free Library." In another endorsement, the librarian of the Free Public Library of Santa Barbara claimed that her rural patrons valued county library service "so strongly as to give the book service a place with rural free mail delivery and [the] telephone among their needs for comfort and best development." The work gained such popularity in Fresno County that a librarian there declared that if terminated, "the country people would rise up, as one people, and mob them [the supervisors]."[43]

Many of the first professionally trained women librarians had to overcome a nineteenth-century stereotype of the librarian's work as

> among the sedentary occupations . . . offering a pleasant
> field for the closing days of broken-down ministers, school
> teachers, aged feminine 'left-overs,' and impoverished
> widows.[44]

Western women librarians contributed to a new image for librarians in several ways. Traveling libraries and library visitors represent just two of the highly successful endeavors that nurtured an interest in and support of the public and county libraries. As they established libraries—permanent educational and moral forces—in western communities, western women librarians shared with men, women, and children their broader vision of the library's role in western society.

~ seven ~

A Professional Watershed

~

THE HIGH WATER
MARK . . . HAS BEEN
REACHED AND THE
PENDULUM HAS
BEGUN TO SWING
THE OTHER WAY.
—MARY FRANCES
ISOM, 1910

Western library development came to a near standstill as the war in Europe escalated. The preceptress of the Wisconsin Library School observed in 1915: "The library world like all the rest of the business world is almost at a stand still and very few positions are appearing on the horizon." Based on the number of requests she received for librarians, Hazeltine concluded that "the West is practically dead." An Oregon librarian shared her pessimistic outlook, observing that "the future looks so dark for Oregon and other western states just now."[1]

As the pioneering phase of western library work began to slow, and library work became more routine, librarians began to reflect upon their personal and professional progress. Those who had entered the profession because of its potential for social service gradually grew disillusioned as it became increasingly bureaucratized. They saw their vision of the library, and all they had worked for, maturing into a marginal cultural institution serving a predominantly middle-class clientele.

American society's growing emphasis on leisure, consumption, and individual attainment contributed to the erosion of librarians' sense of community and their shared vision for the profession. Educated women became "more 'modern' in the sense of greater detachment from tradition and community" and, at the same time, they found it difficult to pinpoint the root of their discontent. Many became painfully conscious of being "satisfied but not contented—or contented but not satisfied." One woman, representative of many, wrote of being "ashamed" to acknowledge her unhappiness. She feared that others would think her "never satisfied."[2]

At the same time, several of the West's most visible library pioneers began to fade from the scene. California State Librarian James L. Gillis died in 1917, and Oregon's Mary Frances Isom and Ida A. Kidder passed away three years later. Both Isom and Kidder continued to work at their libraries during the last few months of their lives, exemplifying the pioneer generation's spirit and commitment to librarianship. Although weak in body, Kidder could not restrain herself physically when mentally she felt "just as I used to, as if I could tear down mountains."[3]

Age also slowed the missionary endeavors of University of Denver librarian Linda M. Clatworthy. A former public library organizer in several western states, she recognized that the time had come to

> find some library workers who are not afraid to give some years to the missionary work . . . I have done mine, tho [sic] I wish I were younger again and could afford to do some more.

Clatworthy feared, however, that because the current generation of library school graduates observed so many librarians engaged in a preponderance of technical work, they might fail to recognize the librarian's potential for social service. Her 1921 address to graduates of the library school at Simmons College admonished them to pursue true library work, "aggressive, missionary work, the kind that does not wait behind the desk for the clock to strike the hour."[4]

Others among the first generation also recognized that their progeny had different motivations, aspirations, and expectations. Cornelia Marvin, who served as Secretary of the Oregon State Library Commission and State Librarian from 1905 until her marriage in 1929, had hoped to see librarians regarded as intellectual leaders and librarianship "placed on a higher plane." Near the end of her career, however, a disillusioned Marvin reflected:

> Twenty-five years ago the situation was very different. There was a pioneer spirit and a missionary spirit, which is, I presume, incidental to all new movements. . . . All the mechanical things which were done were accomplished to clear the way for the great work which was to come. Everyone was hopeful. I do not know just what has happened.[5]

Marvin and others in her generation had performed the mechanical aspects of library work in order to move beyond routine to a more powerful phase of librarianship. It appeared that during the process, the means had obscured, even displaced, the ultimate goal.

Early library school graduates accepted, seemingly without question, the necessity of the "bare mechanical side" of their work, which took "so much time and energy." Carrying their mission to the West, they found opportunities to become leaders—especially as library organizers and in rural public libraries, state agricultural colleges, and normal schools. Once situated, however, they often found themselves in one-person libraries, performing a multitude of professional, clerical, and even janitorial tasks. Such work did not satisfy the high expectations instilled during their library school days.

Succeeding generations of library school graduates grew impatient, restless for work that provided more immediate rewards. Frustrated by days filled by clerical routine, a normal school librarian in Washington concluded:

> I feel that I know how to put on labels and apply shellac
> and ammonia sufficiently well now . . . where no help is
> given the mechanical work takes far too much of the
> librarian's time.[6]

The blurring of professional work and clerical duties led some women, especially those who had chosen this career because of its opportunity for social service, to abandon librarianship altogether. In 1917, a Bakersfield, California, librarian resigned her position, citing that "the work does not appeal to me as library work has always done before." Others felt ashamed of the compromises their inadequate budgets— for assistants, supplies, and books—forced them to make. A Salem, Oregon, woman confided that she could no longer do "good work" because her board did not have enough money. Likewise, a colleague at the Astoria Public Library saw "little more chance of doing any great amount of constructive work without more money than I see in sight." Such limitations proved discouraging, especially to the first generation of professionally trained librarians, because they knew that "so much that might be done if one only had the wherewithal to do it with."[7]

When the western women librarians paused to evaluate their personal lives, many found themselves living in remote locations, isolated from friends and colleagues. As their work became less satisfying, they became increasingly aware of this isolation. In addition to missing the company of friends and family, they suffered professionally by being so far removed from other trained librarians. Lucy Lewis, for example, saw "possibilities for great things in the next few years," and wanted to be in a place "where I would not be so much alone in my line of work." She longed for colleagues with whom she could discuss professional issues. Similar circumstances prompted a rural Oregon librarian to apply for work in Portland: "Contact with people in one's own profession means a good deal."[8] Women who remained for long periods in remote locations also experienced a loss of confidence and self-esteem. One, who eventually accepted another position, confided that she was "dreading the change" because after a number of years in an isolated community, she had begun to doubt her "strength and ability to do things." Finally, others simply tired of rural life. A librarian in Lincoln County, Montana, concluded: "I think I would like to work again in a larger place, county, city, or university library. I would enjoy being again in a university atmosphere. I am tired of Main Street."[9]

Emphasis on service continued to erode as women librarians, like many other Americans, became more consumer-oriented and library salaries remained low. A public librarian in Seattle regretted that her salary would not allow her to purchase an electric toaster and a percolator. And another woman refused a public library position in Washington, informing the state librarian that she would not be able to meet all of her responsibilities "with such a small salary." Correspondence between the graduates and the library school directors reflects both a growing sense of individual worth and increasing discontent with their salaries. Many worked "of economic necessity," but did not wish to remain indefinitely "as an assistant with no advance in salary." Evidence of a growing level of assertiveness appears in one woman's declaration that she expected "to be worth it, or worth nothing for your work" and in another's threat that there would have to be an advance "if she was to remain." Another refused to accept an academic library position when she learned that a professor would retain the title of "librarian" while she, as "Assistant Librarian," would assume full responsibility for the daily operation of the library.[10] And the state librarian in Colorado expressed disgust when the governor vetoed the bill that would have given her a raise:

He evidently thinks that librarians should be paid less than clerks, stenographers, or head janitors, or else cannot get over the fact that I am a Democratic office holder, so [he] prefers to let the status of the librarian's pay remain where it was in 1861, "befo' de wah."[11]

It is little wonder, in an increasingly consumer-oriented society, that librarians tired of giving their best service for inadequate compensation.

At a time when garbage men, wallpaper hangers, and milk wagon drivers struck for ten dollars a day, librarians could expect to earn forty to seventy-five dollars a month. Systematic data for early professional salaries is not readily available (see Table 7.1), but a study of Pratt Institute of Technology Library School alumni, conducted in 1899, reveals that a graduate of that school earned an average annual salary of $686. To qualify for a library position, however, she needed some college education, at least one year of library training, and she often had to serve a probationary period with little or no pay. Her position required approximately forty-two and one-half hours of work each week, forty-eight weeks of the year. By 1913, the outlook had improved somewhat: The salary had risen approximately 36 percent (to $1,081), she worked a forty-hour week, and received, on the average, six weeks of vacation. Meanwhile, the minimum subsistence wage for women living apart from their families, circa 1908–14, ranged from $416 to $520 per year.[12]

It is difficult to compare the earnings of librarians and teachers because the latter often boarded with families and worked only a portion of the year. Although librarians fared substantially better than teachers, in terms of annual compensation, many professionally trained librarians perceived teachers as receiving better salaries and benefits. A normal school librarian observed in 1906 that because "teachers are paid better" librarians needed to "educate the people to believe they must pay for good library service in proportion, at least, as they pay for school service." In 1915, a librarian in the Pacific Northwest wanted to hire an assistant for thirty-five or forty-five dollars a month, but she discovered that "any one who can get a 3rd grade [teaching] certificate can go out and teach for $60.00 a month."[13] Indeed, the librarians' additional education did not appear to yield economic rewards.

Table 7.1 Average Annual Earnings in Real Dollars of Workers in Three
Feminized Professions, 1892–1913

Year	Trained Public Public Health Nurses	Public School Teachers	Professional Librarians (Women Only)
1892	—	$270	$ 570*
1899	—	$318	$ 686
1913	$600–1,020**	$547	$1,081

*Subordinates earned $300-$500; Catalogers earned $699-$900; Head Librarians averaged $1,000 per annum.

**Staff nurses earned $600-$1,020; Supervisors earned $960-$1,020.

Sources: Mary S. Cutler, "What a Woman Librarian Earns," *Library Journal* 17 (Conf. No. 1892): 90; Paul H. Douglas, *Real Wages in the United States, 1890–1926* (Boston: Houghton Mifflin Co., 1930); Josephine Adams Rathbone, "Salaries of Library School Graduates," *Library Journal* 39 (1914): 190; Susan M. Reverby, *Ordered to Care: The Dilemma of American Nursing, 1850–1945* (New York: Cambridge University Press, 1987), p. 108; and U. S. Bureau of the Census, *Historical Statistics of the United States: Colonial Times to 1970*, Part I (Washington: Government Printing Office), p. 168.

The West's geographic beauty and healthful climate had caused some graduates to "make sacrifices in salaries," while others considered the opportunity to work under the direction of prominent library workers "sufficient recompense." Cornelia Marvin elicited the admiration of many: "She is such a splendid woman . . . to work with her has been worth all the sacrifice I made in salary to come here." Finally, others had moved west to be near their families. When the novelty of their positions and the region lessened and work began to provide fewer intrinsic rewards, however, salaries became a higher priority.[14]

After observing numerous "public-spirited" librarians who had accepted the low salaries that many western communities offered, a faculty member at the University of Illinois Library School concluded that they had done themselves and the profession a disservice. Their example had allowed library boards to remain "conservative in regard to salaries." William E. Henry, director of the University of Washington Library School, concurred that one of the profession's chief problems was that its practitioners were willing to accept "less than decent pay."[15]

Library school directors encouraged employers to compensate their librarians adequately, emphasizing that otherwise they would experience high turnover. When one employer asked Los Angeles Public Library director, Charles Lummis, to recommend a librarian who would be willing to work for $40 a month, Lummis responded that he could not "find one person . . . who would take the position." Moreover, if he had such a person he would not attempt "to palm [them] off" on another library.[16] Unfortunately, the precedent set by amateur librarians, who often regarded library work as a temporary past-time rather than a lifelong career, meant that many communities remained unaware of what professional librarians could offer and also what they should be paid.

Librarians in western normal schools and colleges became increasingly unhappy when they learned that women faculty received higher salaries and more extensive benefits than the librarians. That women faculty, in turn, received less than their male counterparts is significant. Even at this early date, librarians ranked at or near the bottom of the salary ladder, an indicator that academic administrators, quickly came to regard librarians as technicians rather than as professionals. Mary Royce Crawford's "professional pride" rebelled after learning that she received "a salary less than assistants in other departments." And it distressed Mabel Reynolds, a teacher turned librarian, to learn that she received "a lower salary than any other woman on the faculty save one, a person of very limited training and experience." She informed her principal that it lowered her position and the work she did "in the eyes of all." She was "ashamed" to find herself "working longer hours than others on the faculty." He did not consider her inefficient or subordinate, however, but informed her that "you do not have to pay librarians" because "whether trained or not, they did the work."[17]

Such conditions led many of the western women librarians to look for new positions, ones more in accord with their professional qualifications and experience:

> One may type cards and file for eight hours a day and
> receive a salary of $100 [per month] . . . but it does not
> quite satisfy when one has had a good deal of experience
> and feels herself fit for a little more work.[18]

The librarians' concern about advancement became a matter of professional pride. Instead of making a long-term commitment to a community and an institution, later generations of library school students openly admitted that they expected to change positions as opportunities arose. They believed that small, rural libraries could not "hold a trained librarian after they have had the experience of a number of months." As one woman wrote, her initial delight had faded, and she "tired of a position that demands so little of me." Another, in Lewiston, Idaho, wanted a change so she would be "somewhere where there is more opportunity for growth."[19]

Women quickly recognized that changing positions also represented the most effective method of improving their individual salaries. Some remained for many years at the same institution, but others did not let loyalty to employers and institutions inhibit their quest for advancement: "They knew that they couldn't hope to keep me long at my present salary." Because so many women expressed interest in upward mobility, library schools began to maintain lists not only of current graduates who needed placement but also of librarians who wished to make a change. Nonetheless, directors cautioned graduates not to change positions too frequently. Upon learning that an Illinois graduate had changed positions again, Frances Simpson chided:

> My only criticism is that you are changing positions rather
> too often for your own good. You know, of course, my
> attitude on that subject. I think it is a mistake for a beginner
> to change positions every year.

Simpson believed that librarians had a duty to "stay long enough in a position to be a real factor in a community." Well aware that library school directors looked with disfavor on those who changed positions too frequently, one woman prefaced a letter announcing her change: "No doubt you have thought that I have changed positions often, but I find that nearly every change has meant advancement in some way." One who had remained in the same position for many years concluded in retrospect that "it would have been better for me had I moved more often."[20]

Educators informed graduate librarians that this practice—of changing positions in order to secure increases in salary—merely perpetuated low salaries in many institutions. When a librarian left her position, library boards and college presidents replaced her, often with a recent graduate who they again paid the starting salary. Frances Simpson, at the University of Illinois Library School, informed Mabel Reynolds that she would be doing a disservice to the profession by leaving her normal school position: "The President would doubtless fill the position with some young graduate who would be glad for $65 or $75." This strategy had its limitations, as librarians gradually discovered. While there were many changes among the ranks of graduates "going from the first to the second salary," changes from the second to the third, and third to fourth positions became progressively slower because positions were fewer and competition intensified.[21]

Education represented an opportunity for upward mobility for some of the western librarians. Those who worked in academic libraries took advantage of opportunities to take classes, while others occasionally left their employment to return to school where they completed bachelor's degrees, earned master's degrees, or took additional library school course work. Librarians at the University of Wyoming and the University of Denver found that their "short hours" enabled them to take classes. Gladys Germand's six-hour work day in Laramie enabled her to carry a course load that included "eight and one-half hours college work—psychology, history, English, and an evening class in gymnasium work." Corine Kittelson took advantage of the classes that the University of Denver offered teachers on Saturday:

> The Denver University offers good opportunity in their
> Saturday classes for teachers, to all those aspiring for this
> degree. . . . This has not in any way been urged upon me
> . . . but I am ambitious to gain all I can. My short hours will
> make this possible.[22]

Charlotte Baker, Belle Sweet, and Ida Kidder represent just a few library directors who enthusiastically supported their assistants when they requested time away from the library to attend classes. Library school directors also rejoiced to learn that their former students planned to continue their education. Mary E. Hazeltine wrote to one protégée of her delight in learning that the young woman's "dreams are at last to come true."[23]

Women who worked in one-person libraries, however, seldom could spare the time required to take classes. Nonetheless, they continued to improve themselves by attending lectures, musicals, and exhibits. Some pursued correspondence courses, while others arranged for leaves of absence so they could return to school on a full-time basis. Illinois students who had left that school after their junior year to take positions sometimes returned to complete the course. Florence Waller, a librarian at the State College of Washington, explained that after obtaining practical experience, she had "accumulated a mass of questions that even a year's school can't answer."[24] Women who had completed a general library school course sometimes entered another school in pursuit of more specialized training. Several, for example, enrolled in the Training School for Children's Librarians in Pittsburgh, where they specialized in children's work. Librarians thoroughly enjoyed their school days and sometimes found it difficult to return to their former positions: "But oh, it was a glorious year! I wanted to stay on for another nine months to get my Master's degree."[25] Thus, women who wanted to improve their status or professional prospects had at least two options: They could change positions, or they could use education as a springboard to new opportunities.

America's entrance into World War I, however, provided librarians with another opportunity for service. As library work became more routine, and the organizing frenzy of the previous decade waned, so did some women's enthusiasm for librarianship. But the war "helped deepen the public library's sense of mission, and increased its claim to legitimacy as a viable local community resource."[26] It provided a new way for librarians to demonstrate the library's unique role in the preservation of democracy. Thus, it was in this war-minded climate that many western librarians and libraries engaged in the war effort. Some worked within their local communities, others participated in the American Library Association's War Service Work by serving in camp libraries and in Washington, D.C., and a few went overseas.

At the local level, librarians found several ways to participate in the war effort. The librarian of the Fort Collins, Colorado, Public Library, spread war posters throughout her library. In Spokane, Washington, the library staff collected more than fifteen thousand books from within the city, which they then distributed to Camp Lewis and to a distributing station in Portland. Additionally, the library prepared a "war food exhibit" in the lobby of the central library. Librarians cooked the sample foods in the staff kitchen, under the direction of a dietician, and changed the exhibit daily. They also distributed thou-

7.1. World War I posters in the Fort Collins, Colorado, Public Library.
Courtesy Fort Collins Public Library

sands of multigraphed collections of recipes to men and women who
visited the library. The Spokane librarians also entered a memorable
float in the Red Cross parade in May 1918. It depicted a nurse reading
to a wounded soldier, and two platoons of women library staff followed,
dressed as nurses. They marched behind a librarian dressed as a soldier
and carrying a stack of books.[27]

Elsewhere, librarians used library lawns to demonstrate additional
ways of supporting the war effort. A librarian in Canon City, Colorado,
reported that she and her staff had "plowed up a good space [on the
library's lot], and have planted it to vegetables." Librarians also
opened their libraries for public meetings and ran Americanization
programs that included the preparation of bibliographies and development of special services tailored to foreign populations.[28]

Other western women librarians requested leave from their library
positions to volunteer for War Service Work. Grace Raymond Hebard's
work piled up on her desk at the University of Wyoming during the

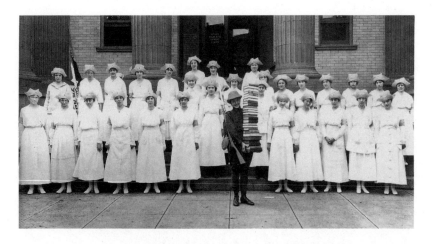

7.2. The Spokane Public Library Staff, Red Cross Parade, May 1918.
Courtesy Spokane Public Library

time she was in Washington, D.C. Meanwhile, one of her assistants delayed reporting to work because of her involvement "on the Mexican Border in connection with Libraries for Camps." Although many women sought ways to contribute to the war effort, they also recognized that the war created well-paid positions for librarians at a time when the job market waned: "There is such a demand for cataloguers to fill government positions at large salaries."[29]

Ida Kidder saw evidence of the war everywhere she looked. Young men on the campus of the Oregon State Agricultural College marched and women sewed clothing for French orphans in the dormitories. Kidder described the dormitory women as "just crazy over the idea of adopting an orphan." She also became so deeply absorbed in "thinking about these darling French orphans" that she suffered a fall. Kidder's visit to the "boys" in Company K at Camp Lewis in Washington fueled her desire to provide them with good reading material that would save them "from idleness, great loneliness and perhaps vices." She believed that as an "old and staid" woman, she would be an especially effective camp librarian because "those young men need no feminine diversion, their minds should be upon the work they are learning and the future they face."[30] Finally, Mary Frances Isom directed the American Library Association's war work in Oregon and southern Washington, devoted herself to Liberty Bond drives, and served in France from November 1918 to April 1919.

The year 1917 does appear to represent a watershed, both in the history of the profession and in western librarianship. Prior to America's entrance into the war, the American Library Association's motto had been "the best reading for the largest number at the least cost." By concentrating on efficiency and organization, the profession could, by 1917, point with pride to hundreds of systematically organized libraries efficiently managed by professional librarians who provided reference service, information for special populations (that is, children, immigrants, the institutionalized), instruction in the use of the library, and library extension. As the cultural crusaders began to fade from the scene, however, those who replaced them inherited the routine without the exhilaration of the pioneering era. America's entrance into World War I restored—albeit temporarily—flagging professional zeal by providing librarians with a new frontier.

~ eight ~

Four Who Served

Western librarianship provided an arena in which the cultural crusaders could develop successful careers as well as a system of libraries and services. While few could be categorized as radical feminists, they did blend feminist ideals with rational values and an ethic of caring as they extended their spheres of influence throughout the region. Operating within the constraints of time, place, and gender, they transcended female stereotypes as they pursued their vision of library service. This chapter focuses on four who exemplify the spirit of the cultural crusaders. Arranged chronologically by birthdate, the lives of these four provide a basis for revaluing and reclaiming women's professional past.

Ida Angeline Clarke Kidder, 1857–1920

Born in Auburn, New York, on June 30, 1857, Ida Angeline Clarke graduated from high school in Waverly, New York, at the age of twenty. She enrolled in the New York State College for Teachers in Albany nine years later. During the interim she served as a primary teacher in Waverly (1878–85), and after her year at the normal school she became a teacher of natural sciences, and ultimately principal, of the Medina, New York, High School (1887–95). Her teaching career ended at age thirty-nine with her marriage to Lorenzo Kidder.

Information about Kidder's married life is elusive, but it appears that the couple had no children. By 1905 Kidder, presumably a widow, had enrolled in the University of Illinois Library School, from which she graduated in 1906. Somewhat older than her classmates, she wore her hair in a tight little bun at the top of her head and gained the affectionate nickname "Mama Katzenjammer." From Illinois, she traveled West to become a library organizer in Washington (1906) and Oregon (1907–8). Katharine Sharp had predicted that Kidder would "make a good field worker for some commission. . . . Her maturity, club work and successful teaching experience are all in her favor."

8.1. "Mother Kidder." Courtesy Oregon State University (Harriet's Collection #265)

Sharp's high praise of her student led Cornelia Marvin to write, "I should particularly like to have Mrs. Kidder out here."

When Kidder finally reached Oregon, her duties were varied:

> I do all sorts of things, visit Teachers' institutes to tell them about the care and use of school libraries . . . visit farmers' institutes to tell them about traveling libraries . . . help schools in cataloging their libraries, make the catalog for normal school libraries, help public libraries, take care of the penitentiary catalog, and anything else that can be thought of to help the library cause. In a state so large and new as Oregon, it is pioneering.

Kidder recognized that hiring a field worker represented a great expense for a fledgling commission, but after she spent several years traveling great distances by stage, boat, and train to promote the library cause, she remained convinced that "causes are advanced only through individuals . . . I do not see how people are to be interested in books and libraries any other way."

By the time the Oregon State Library Commission could no longer fund a field worker, Kidder had grown "so fond of this far west that I do not want to leave it." In the spring of 1908, the president of the Oregon State Agricultural College in Corvallis decided to appoint that institution's first professionally trained librarian and he called upon Kidder. She reflected:

> They [OAC] need some very strong body to carry them out
> to success and people always seem to think I am a strong
> body, though I sometimes get awfully tired of being strong,
> don't you? Still, I believe with Emerson that there are
> compensations.

Bringing her vitality, spirit, and interest in young people to the one-room library in Benton Hall, the college librarian soon became known by students as "Mother Kidder."

Kidder, like many other female academic librarians of this era, lived in a dormitory and took her "social recreation with the students." She even learned to dance "a little" after she discovered the Oregonians to be "perfect fiends for dancing." Indeed, she found it difficult to turn down the many social invitations she received, believing that "perhaps, after all, the best work I am doing in the world is touching the lives of individuals, of some of our students . . . touching the real springs of action."

Even though she became an academic librarian, Kidder never relinquished her interest in public library development. The months she had spent working as a commission organizer had left a deep impression. Kidder believed that the agricultural college library "should do all that is reasonable and within its power to stimulate the public library in its work for the state." In addition to working on behalf of the public library movement in Corvallis, she canvassed the state, speaking about the value of libraries and the value of reading in the home. Kidder believed in the personal touch:

> It is the touch of a warm personality which alone can fire
> the hearts of other men. The great advance of the world has

been made by great warm-hearted wise people clasping
hands with the weak and leading them upward.

Faculty, students, and assistants in the library all praised Kidder's
charismatic, energetic personality. They saw her as congenial and progressive, an "'ideal librarian': Nothing escapes her notice that will aid
in any way in building up the library, and she is tireless in carrying out
these ideas." Mrs. Kidder, considered a "born teacher," provided instruction in the use of the library, did the administrative work, and
performed the "heavier reference work." As her staff grew, she delegated the loan work, cataloging, and extension work.

In 1911 Kidder recruited Lucy Lewis to become her assistant librarian. The two had been classmates during their library school days
at the University of Illinois and had remained in close touch since that
time. As librarians of agricultural college libraries, both shared many
ideas about their profession. Lewis, after several years in Las Cruces,
New Mexico, sought a change of scenery and welcomed this opportunity to join her friend. Kidder, in her mid-fifties at the time, suffered
from arthritis and a cardiac ailment that made it increasingly difficult
to walk. Unwilling to give up her active lifestyle, she obtained a wicker
electric cart that students christened the "Kidder Car" or the "Wickermobile," that she drove all over campus.

Eager to assist in the war effort, Kidder left Lewis in charge of the
college library and spent the summer of 1918 as a hospital librarian at
Camp Lewis, Washington. Reflecting on this experience, she recalled
that "in most cases they [the soldiers] needed a mother as much as a
doctor." She took delight in seeing "how they would brighten up and
take new heart of courage at the appearance of a lame, gray-haired
woman, who came to them with a motherly spirit in her heart." Indeed, they also came to call her "Mother Kidder." Her sobriquet
became so well-known that a soldier's letter, addressed only to
"Mother Kidder, Oregon," reached her desk in Corvallis. "Dear
Mother," wrote another young soldier in France, "don't you dare call
yourself 'old.' That applies only to people who have ceased to be
interesting . . . not to such dynamos of kindness, sympathy and understanding as you." He continued:

Mother, you will never get old, for the companionship of
your incorruptible boys and girls and the immortals that live

8.2. Ida A. Kidder in her "wickermobile," ca. 1918.
Courtesy Oregon State University Archives (P3:6496)

on your bookshelves has endowed you with a personality
that defies the march of time.

Kidder maintained a voluminous correspondence with former students, librarians, educators, journalists, and many others. All who knew her commented on her vibrant, dynamic personality. A year before her death, she reviewed her life and looked to the future. Observing that "life grows more mysterious and more incomprehensible with every passing year," Kidder admitted that she was "anxious to know what death means," and that she planned to approach it as she had life— "cheerfully and happily."

Ida A. Kidder served as librarian of the Oregon State Agricultural College for twelve years, and saw her dream of a new library building realized in 1911. As her health worsened, her enthusiasm for librarianship grew stronger. In 1918, after returning from giving a speech at the Harrisburg Public Library, she wrote: "Oh! I am so stirred up on the public library question that I want to go out on a crusade. . . . So blessed are we to have a great work to do and one that we love." Two years later, in January 1920, a recurrence of heart trouble forced her to request a leave of absence. Ida A. Kidder passed away on February 29, 1920, and her body lay in state in the library that later bore her name.[1]

8.3. Mary Frances Isom, 1865–1920.
Courtesy Portland, Multonomah County Library

Mary Frances Isom, 1865–1920

Born in Nashville, Tennessee, on February 27, 1865, where her father served as an army surgeon, Mary Frances Isom grew to adulthood in Cleveland, Ohio. Her mother passed away a few years before she entered Wellesley in 1883, and the young woman became increasingly devoted to her father. After only a year at Wellesley, ill health caused Isom to return to Cleveland where she served as a hostess for and companion to her father until his death in 1899.

Even though her father's death left her financially independent and able to live a life of leisure, Isom chose a life of service. With the encouragement of a childhood friend, Josephine Adams Rathbone, she traveled to Brooklyn, New York, to enroll in the Pratt Institute Library School. Upon completion of the program in the spring 1901, she returned briefly to Cleveland before accepting a position in Portland, Oregon. There she began cataloging a collection of books bequeathed to the Library Association of Portland. Soon after her arrival, the board of this private subscription library decided to open it to the public. When the head librarian departed in January 1902, the board elected Isom in his place, and by the following year the once restrictive collection was accessible to every citizen in Multnomah County.

In 1904 Isom's call for a meeting of Oregonians who supported the advancement of library service in the state resulted in the organization of the Oregon Library Association. She also helped persuade the American Library Association (ALA) to hold its 1905 annual conference in Portland. She and a number of others within the profession believed that the ALA meeting would stimulate public interest in libraries in Oregon and throughout the West.

State library associations had a difficult time attaining the critical mass necessary to sustain their meetings. Eager to see a sense of community grow among western librarians, Isom helped organize the Pacific Northwest Library Association in 1909. She confided to Cornelia Marvin that her loyalty lay with the state and regional associations: "You know I am still a Philistine as regard the ALA. . . . I think that a small association that is alive is more important for our people than the larger." Nonetheless, her colleagues throughout the country held her in high esteem, electing her to American Library Association Council, and in 1912–13, they chose her to serve as the association's second vice president.

Viewing the public library as "the people's library," Isom devoted much time and energy to work with children and immigrants. She worked to establish closer cooperation with the public schools, and by 1920 the Central Library and its branches served nearly 150 schools. Eager to see immigrant families use the library, she nonetheless acknowledged their customs and invited them to share their cultural traditions at library programs. Isom filled her library with a spirit of service as she devoted her career to bringing books and people to-gether. One man, unused to such excellent reference service, told Isom: "Look here, girlie, you don't need to shine up to me, it won't get you nowhere."

The Portland librarian wanted to see library service made available to every citizen in the state. Working with Sarah Evans, head of the Oregon Federation of Women's Clubs, she campaigned successfully on behalf of legislation that would establish, in 1905, the State Library Commission and a school library law. In her capacity as member of the newly created State Library Commission (a position she held until her death), Isom recruited Cornelia Marvin to become secretary of the State Library Commission.

Isom remained somewhat distant from her employees, and even her close friend and colleague, Cornelia Marvin, described her rela-tions with her staff as "entirely impersonal." Although she regularly corrected employees, and firmly believed in discipline and organiza-tion, she nevertheless cared deeply about their welfare. One story re-counts how she appeared before a young employee on Christmas Eve, saying "You have a family. I have none. Go home and enjoy the holi-day." Concern for her employees also led Isom to bequeath five thou-sand dollars to be used as the beginning of a pension fund for the staff.

Marvin, who spent many leisure hours with Isom, described her friend as "never afraid of anything." On a picnic, when they encoun-tered bulls running loose, Isom "called to them instead of being afraid . . . she took everything as it came." Isom entertained frequently, holding Sunday "at-homes." When she first arrived in Portland she lived in a hotel or apartment, but later she built "a beautiful artistic house with large fenced grounds" where she entertained "interesting Portland and Oregon people and visiting librarians." The income from her father's estate also made it possible for her to maintain a beach cottage, named "Spindrift," designed for her by architect Albert Doyle. There she enjoyed long walks on the beach with her bull terrier, Bunker Hill, who also spent many days in her office at the library. Although she remained single, Isom adopted a ten-year-old child, Ber-nice, the daughter of a Cleveland friend.

During World War I, Isom became ALA's director of War Work in Oregon and southern Washington. She also organized hospital and camp libraries. Additionally, she devoted her energy to Liberty Bond drives. When the refusal of her assistant librarian, M. Louise Hunt, to buy bonds (because of her pacifist convictions) became a public issue, Isom stood firm and rejected demands that she be dismissed. As a result, her own patriotism came under fire. This may, in part, explain why, during the last months of the war, Isom accepted an invitation for war service in France. Arriving in November 1918, the fifty-three-year-old librarian was anxious to be of use: "Put me wherever you need me." She spent countless hours in wards, carrying books to soldiers, who she described as demoralized by the idleness that accompanied the armistice. Many of the scenes disturbed, but also seasoned Isom, and in a letter to her staff in Portland she confided: "I can stand anything now. I can even look on the most horrible wounds without flinching."

Isom's overseas services ended abruptly, when a pain in her arm, diagnosed as cancer, forced her return home early in 1919. Back in Portland, however, she refused to remain abed, and spent several hours each day at the library until two weeks before her death, which occurred on April 15, 1920.[2]

Charlotte A. Baker, 1867–1947

Charlotte A. Baker's parents, William Van Ness and Sarah Frances Terry Baker, moved to Troy, New York, two years after her birth in Racine, Wisconsin, on May 15, 1867. She received her education at the Troy Female Seminary, later known as the Emma Willard School, and from private teachers. Graduating from New York State College for Teachers in Albany in 1891, she expected to teach but a physical breakdown, and a diagnosis of tuberculosis, led her to seek a drier climate. Even after a year at Saranac Lake, doctors estimated that Baker had only a year or two to live. Thus, in 1893, she and her sister, Anna, moved to Colorado in search of a more healthful climate.

Once there, Baker became a special student at Colorado College, intending to prepare for a career as a high school teacher of mathematics. After suffering another breakdown, however, Baker concluded: "I could never earn my living in an occupation that required constant use of my voice." Library work appeared to be better suited for a woman with her physical limitations, so Baker traveled to Denver where she took the entrance examinations for the Denver Public Library Training Class. Upon completion of the course in 1894, she

8.4. Denver Public Library staff, East High School, ca. 1895–1900, with Charlotte A. Baker (center back). Courtesy Denver Public Library, Western History Department

joined the staff. Training-class students represented a cheap source of labor. Students at the Denver Public Library received nothing for six months, then five dollars per month afterward. This led Baker to observe that "library work was genteel work for girls who lived at home and wanted pin money." Baker, however, lived with her sister, and laundered her own shirtwaists "in order to present the proper appearance which library work required but which library salaries did not allow her to obtain from a laundry."

Soon after she joined the staff of the Denver Public Library, an accident reportedly triggered a recurrence of tuberculosis, this time "tuberculosis of the bones." As a result, Baker, who from time to time depended upon crutches, settled into a relatively sedentary position cataloging books and teaching literature to successive groups of training class students.

After several years had passed, Baker grew stronger and restless. Desiring another change, she moved with her sister to Las Cruces, New Mexico, in July 1900, where she became librarian of the New Mexico College of Agriculture and Mechanic Arts. Hence began her long career as a land-grant college librarian. The Spanish-American community of Las Cruces, according to Baker, had "but two buildings that were two stories high, the rest of the town being adobe structures." The college consisted of a few brick buildings in addition to adobe dwellings, but it had "no sewage, no lights, no pavements." The landscape was dotted with windmills, and for fuel Baker recalled burning wood hauled in from the mountains. As a trained librarian, Baker felt like a novelty on campus, especially because the administrators used to "exhibit" her to visitors.

The library room had three doors, two used as entrances to the library and one a private entrance to the "librarian's cage." Baker soon became frustrated because the counter had no opening and the librarian had to exit into the hall and enter through another door if she wanted access to the main part of the library. The president denied Baker's request "to have a little hole made for me to get out" because he did not want to spoil the counter's beautiful wood. A short while later, recalled Baker, the president "came into the library one day just in time to see me vault over the counter into the main part of the room." After he reprimanded her for her undignified behavior, Baker made it a point to drop "everything when I heard him come down the hall, and he always found me just flying over the counter. The hole was cut."

While in New Mexico, a robust Baker claimed that her "avocations were dancing and horseback riding," and she took excursions as far south as Veracruz. As a "city woman who was new in a country community," she sometimes suffered from pranks, but fortunately, Baker had never "been afraid of mice, and horned toads, and I do not mind a snake, if it is not poked back of my ear." She enjoyed being in Las Cruces during the "frisky period of its existence," but by 1906 she was ready to forsake pioneer life for Colorado, "a land of closets, electric lights and bath tubs."

When she left Las Cruces, Baker became an assistant librarian at the Colorado State Agricultural College in Fort Collins. After head librarian Joseph Daniels departed for California in 1910, she succeeded him. Always known for saying what was on her mind, Baker's blunt tongue and colorful personality earned her a reputation as a "character." Affectionately nicknamed by the students as "Ma Baker," she imbued in her staff the idea that librarianship at its best is a service. She advocated a broad conception of the library's role in an educational institution and helped plan an outstanding academic library building, completed in 1927.

Because of her eagerness to see librarians of the state advance,

Baker worked tirelessly to revive the Colorado Library Association, and held the position of president in 1912–13. Additionally, she served as secretary of the Colorado State Library Commission from 1913 to 1919, and edited the "Occasional Leaflet" from 1913 to 1921. The latter helped her maintain close ties with many of the state's small-town librarians. In her spare time and during her vacations Baker visited the state's public libraries, providing advice and encouragement to many untrained library workers. These visits increased her awareness of the lack of adequate training available to small-town librarians, and led her to develop and direct the "Aggie Library Summer School" from 1918 to 1932. Never one to be idle, Baker continued her own education, earning a B.S. degree from the Colorado Agricultural College in 1928. She retired in 1936, and passed away eleven years later. Reflecting on her life, Baker wrote in 1940:

> Like all people who have more of life behind them than ahead, I find I have not carried out the plans of my youth. On the other hand, I have come to believe that, even with varying health, one may be happy and useful in any community. It is merely making up one's mind to take life as it comes.

In 1914, Chalmers Hadley, librarian of the Denver Public Library attempted to capture the essence of his long-time friend in a playful mock obituary:

> *Under this sod*
> *And under this taper*
> *Lieth the body*
> *of Charlotte A. Baker.*
> *She is not in this hole,*
> *But only her pod.*
> *She shelled out her soul*
> *and went to her God.*[3]

Mary Belle Sweet, 1879–1964

Mary Belle Sweet was born on January 5, 1879, in Gardenplain, Illinois, but her family moved to northwestern Iowa during her child-

8.5. Mary Belle Sweet, Librarian, University of Idaho.
Courtesy University of Idaho Historical Photograph Collection (#10–89)

hood years. Her father owned a general merchandise store in O'Brien County, but sold it to purchase a farm. Unable to resist an urge to move West, he then relocated to Idaho alone while his wife and daughters moved to Clinton, Iowa, to be near relatives.

Convinced that there "was no place in Idaho where you could go to school," Sweet's father insisted that she and her sister remain in Iowa to complete their education. The Clinton High School had a small library managed by "a very wonderful woman"—the wife of the superintendent of schools—and she invited Belle to assist her with the library work. Through this experience, and by reading library periodicals, Belle learned that trained librarians "could do better." Because she recognized, from an early age, that "I would have my living to earn," Sweet decided to attend college, and ultimately library school.

Graduating from high school in Clinton, Iowa, in 1897, Sweet taught for two years before matriculating at the University of Wisconsin in 1899. After two years, she left to enter the University of Illinois Library School. Although disappointed that she could not afford to attend the New York State Library School in Albany, she took consolation in knowing that the University of Illinois Library School was "the second best" in the nation.

Sweet graduated from the University of Illinois with a B.L.S. in 1904, and immediately became librarian of her hometown library in Clinton. By December of that year, however, she knew that "it will not be for the good of the library or for my own good . . . to stay here another year." Evidently, the president of the board opposed her actions and "tried to kill her spirit." On the basis of a visit to Clinton in March 1905, the secretary of the Iowa Library Commission concluded that it would not do to send another person with such a "gentle and yielding nature" to Clinton because she would "be harassed in a manner similar to Miss Sweet." Sweet tendered her resignation, believing that the board of trustees would "have more confidence in a stranger." Her difficulty had been in convincing the board that she was not on the same plane as a "department store clerk," but was instead the executive officer of a public institution.

In 1905, Sweet joined her family, now living in Grangeville, Idaho. Her uncle, Edward S. Sweet, a member of the Board of Regents of the University of Idaho, obtained an interview for her with the president of the university, and she reported to work that fall. Shortly after she took charge of the unclassified collection housed in two rooms of the Administration Building, a fire destroyed the entire building and most of its contents. Sweet recalled that "not much could be saved . . . because they were so afraid that the Chemistry Department would have many things that might explode and it was in the basement, underneath the Library."

Sweet wasted no time in reopening the library the following Monday in the school gymnasium. She began to rebuild her collection first, with a shipment of government documents and newspapers that arrived in that day's mail, and then with gifts. The University of Idaho library remained in the gymnasium for over a year, and basketball games made it difficult for Sweet to keep order: "There would be a heap of books on the floor after the games and they had to be sorted and put back as soon as possible to keep the pages together."

Sweet took part in a number of social activities at the university and in the community. Each fall the unmarried faculty gave a picnic and hayride for all newcomers. Sweet observed that "most of the women who came here didn't know how to cook," so after several disasters, the "custom of having the unmarried people give the party died a natural death." She also attended student dances, and served as a chaperon for the students. Little is known about her personal life. An obituary notes that she and an unmarried sister "reared an adopted daughter," and that her hobbies included "cookie baking, especially during the Christmas season, sewing, and art."

One university president described Sweet as a "packrat" because she "made it a point to take everything that came our way even if it seemed to have no value at the moment." New faculty often came to the University of Idaho expecting it to "be just like the big university from which they came," but Sweet knew that "it couldn't be. . . . Every dollar had to do the work of three or four." An entrepreneur, Sweet instituted charges for at least one library service. Students continually filled their fountain pens, and the library could not afford to provide the ink, so Sweet "put in this filler and for two pennies they could fill their fountain pen. And we made a little money on it . . . and we used that money to buy things."

After nearly ten years of struggling with limited resources, Sweet admitted to being discouraged and restless. In 1916–17 she took a much-need leave of absence, during which time she

> took some work in the secretarial school and some courses
> in English literature and in modern drama. . . . Having lived
> in a small town for a number of years I also felt the need of
> devoting a part of my time to things of general cultural
> value such as the opera, the theatre, various libraries, and
> art museums.

She also did substitute work in the Seattle Public Library for a few months, hoping that experience there would help her find another position "either immediately or later." In the fall of 1917, however, she returned to the University of Idaho, where she served as librarian until her retirement in 1948. Throughout her career, she continued to praise her colleagues at the University of Idaho while lambasting the state legislature for its failure to provide adequate financial support for higher education. When Sweet passed away in Portland at the age of eighty-five, colleagues recalled her as "a hardworking woman, painstaking and conscientious, almost to a fault . . . able to make the best use of her advantages." Throughout her life, Sweet had done just that.[4]

~ *Conclusion* ~

Daughters of the Progressive Era, and products of a middle-class milieu, the first professionally trained librarians in the West shared a vision of the library as a powerful educational agency that could preserve democracy and eradicate social ills. Early library schools fostered and encouraged their altruistic impulses by infusing them with the "library spirit" and the sense of enthusiasm and missionary zeal that typically accompanies newly organized professions. Cornelia Marvin, along with countless others, viewed the West as a tabula rasa, a place where she could exercise professional and personal autonomy. After about 1910, however, librarians increasingly began to regard western positions as opportunities for adventure, advancement, or as temporary assignments that enabled them to see a new and interesting region. Like many Americans, they expected to earn higher salaries in the West than they did in libraries of the eastern United States.

The move west granted a number of these women physical, if not emotional, distance from the family claim. Women of this era often moved west because of a decision made by a husband or father, but most of these librarians made a conscious choice to seek western employment. Indeed, western positions offered many their first taste of independent living. For some, however, the family remained a potent factor shaping the direction of their lives. Several women traveled west accompanied by mothers, fathers, or siblings, and others relocated near relatives. While few librarians married, several of those who remained single created their own families by adopting children. Finally, a number of graduate librarians appear to have regarded library school directors as maternal substitutes. Surviving correspondence provides ample testimony to the library educators' efforts to nurture their graduates as they constructed their lives in the American West.

As single working women in western communities, these librarians discovered that a sense of isolation accompanied their independence. Feeling displaced in communities populated largely by families and single men, academic librarians found companions within their institutions. Women who worked in rural areas, however, had fewer opportunities to interact with other professionals. Librarians in both settings retained a strong sense of connectedness to their eastern colleagues and teachers. Although they spoke enthusiastically about western hospitality, especially in letters written shortly after their arrival, graduate librarians longed for the cultural advantages of eastern cities and for the companionship of women who shared similar interests and aspirations. Some participated in community organizations, for example, churches and women's clubs, but they seldom became part of local female subcultures. Instead, they tended to remain aloof. Perhaps they feared that familiarity with local women would jeopardize their cause, or they may have felt discomfort when interacting socially with the men and women who served as library trustees. Finally, a few librarians expressed feelings of superiority, describing local residents as pretentious or ignorant. For a variety of reasons, then, many of these women found it difficult to fit comfortably into the social fabric of western community life.

During the early years, western women librarians filled their lonesome hours by immersing themselves in work. As time passed, however, and their numbers increased, they began to construct a complex web of supportive colleagues. Although separated by many miles, they sustained each other through frequent correspondence, occasional visits, and encounters at regional and state library association meetings. Librarians in larger communities, for example, Los Angeles, Portland, Seattle, and Spokane, formed local organizations that served as social outlets.

As women entering an occupation that had only recently professionalized, these librarians had to overcome existing stereotypes and practices, even in the West. During much of the nineteenth century, the term librarian had been synonymous with custodian, and the prevailing stereotype of a librarian depicted a sedentary male, possibly a distinguished scholar or someone who either had failed in or retired from another field. Moreover, American public libraries had a long tradition of relying on volunteer or amateur labor to open the library a few hours each week so readers could exchange books. This practice persisted for many years in rural communities, and is evident even today.

Prior to the librarians' arrival in the West, club women had established the rudiments of library service when they collected books, opened reading rooms, and served as volunteer librarians. Eager to provide their children with the advantages they had known in the East and Midwest, these women lacked the professional vision and knowledge that could transform passive collections of books into influential cultural agencies. Sometimes they also succumbed to factionalism and competing demands for their attention. Nonetheless, club women exerted a strong influence within their communities and on their husbands, many of them civic leaders with the power to allocate money to the library cause. The most successful library organizers forged a collaboration with club women, both at the local and state levels, and this powerful feminine alliance lobbied successfully for the passage of library legislation in several western states.

Western librarians faced the dual challenge of legitimating a recently organized field and forging new ground as professional women. Contrary to the pervasive twentieth-century stereotype of the librarian as an introverted, bookish spinster, western women librarians had to be socially adept in order to secure widespread support for a library movement in its infancy. They also needed to be articulate, comfortable with diverse audiences, and prepared to mount a horse, as well as a public podium, with confidence.

The very process of initiating library service in western communities placed these women in a masculine milieu and increased their social, political, and economic awareness and abilities. They worked with local women to advance their cause, but western librarians—especially library organizers—also had frequent interaction with the male civic leaders who controlled local finances. Although librarianship appeared to be compatible with traditional expectations of women, many discovered that western library work provided them with a significant degree of flexibility and autonomy. As they traversed the countryside explaining the library cause to farmers, lumbermen, miners, and ranchers, they extended the boundaries of women's sphere. The experiences of Mabel Wilkinson in Wyoming and of Mabel Prentiss and Bertha Kumli in California represent only a few examples of librarians living and working in a male-dominated terrain. They did not forsake their femininity, however, and on occasion resorted to flirtation and a demeanor of dependence if they thought it advantageous or politically wise.

Geographic barriers, sparse settlement, and strong competition for limited resources fostered innovation and creative adaptation, as exemplified by the work of library organizers and the development of the county library system. Librarians quickly learned the necessity of honing political skills, and they used a variety of public forums, for example, town council meetings, farmers' and teachers' institutes, the pulpit, and the press, to publicize the library's mission and services. Although they worked with a largely literate West, one that could read the Roman alphabet, it is difficult to label them as cultural imperialists. They did attempt to provide foreign-language materials and to reach diverse audiences. Working in tandem with local residents, they recreated library services that many western residents had previously enjoyed in the East. Although they sometimes questioned their public's reading tastes, the librarians usually tried to accommodate them, recognizing that recreational reading provided western residents with respite from difficult lives in isolated areas.

Fueled by their desire to connect books and readers, these women established an efficient and well-managed system of library service in many of the western states. But over time, limited resources did hinder their effectiveness, and also made it difficult for them to exist as independent women in an increasingly consumer-oriented society. Many became frustrated and disillusioned when their positions failed to provide professional or personal satisfaction. Some expressed bitterness and resentment, regret that they had not chosen another line of work, and feelings of being trapped. Others continually changed positions as they sought satisfactory compensation—both economic and in the form of recognition.

The first professionally trained women librarians in the West placed little value on the acquisition of individual power. Instead, they viewed themselves as agents of an influential institution that would empower western citizens. The irony of their success is twofold. First, the institution that they had established did not foster the altruistic spirit in their professional progeny. Second, the institutional stability that resulted from their dedication and hard work produced a hierarchical, patriarchal organization. Ultimately, they, like women librarians in other sections of the country, would find themselves occupying the lower rungs of a bureaucratic ladder. Indeed, as additional research would reveal, men succeeded a number of these women when they retired. By 1917, much of the basic organizational work had been accomplished and a preponderance of clerical-level tasks remained. As altruistic impulses waned, modern women began to replace the Progressive-era generation. Those who remained loyal to the ideology of service found themselves out of step with the profession and even with American culture.

Many of the institutions that these women established survive today. Unfortunately, a number of the barriers and obstacles that challenged them have survived as well. Additional factors—the loss of a sense of community, a society that undervalues women, and the dehumanizing aspects of technology—cause individuals to question their commitment to a service ethic. Perhaps by looking at these cultural crusaders, active agents of their own history, we may gain insight into the personal and professional philosophy that transformed them and left western communities with an enduring legacy.

∼ *Notes* ∼

Abbreviations Used

CAB   Charlotte A. Baker Papers, University Archives, Colorado State University, Fort Collins, Colorado.

CLA   California Library Association Correspondence, California State Archives, Sacramento, California.

CLC   Carnegie Library Correspondence, Microfilm Reels, Carnegie Corporation, New York.

CLFC   County Library Files Correspondence, California State Library Correspondence, F3616, California State Archives, Sacramento.

CLOF   County Library Organizer's Files, F3616, California State Library Correspondence, California State Archives, Sacramento.

CSLC   California State Library Correspondence, F3616, California State Archives, Sacramento.

DEN   Special Collections Department, Penrose Library, University of Denver.

DPLA   Denver Public Library Archives, Western History Department, Denver Public Library, Denver, Colorado.

GRH   Grace Raymond Hebard Papers, American Heritage Center, University of Wyoming, Laramie.

IFLC   Idaho Free Library Commission, Correspondence, Idaho State Library, Boise.

ISL   Indiana State Library, Correspondence, L971, Indiana State Archives, Indianapolis.

JFA   James F. Ailshie Papers, RG9, Special Collections Department, University of Idaho, Moscow.

KLS   Katharine L. Sharp Papers, University of Illinois Archives, Urbana.

LLC   League of Library Commissions, Correspondence, Series 1090, State Historical Society of Wisconsin, Madison.

LSAF   Library School Alumni File, University of Illinois Archives, Urbana.

LSDL   Library School Director's Letterpress, University of Illinois Archives, Urbana.

LSSR   Library School Student Record, University Archives, University of Wisconsin-Madison.

MBS   Mary Belle Sweet Papers, Special Collections Department, University of Idaho, Moscow.

MCPL   Multnomah County Public Library, Administrative Archives, Portland, Oregon.

MDPC   Melvil Dewey Personal Correspondence, Rare Books and Manuscripts Library, Columbia University Libraries, New York, New York.

NSLC   Nebraska State Library Commission, RG16, Nebraska State Historical Society, Lincoln.

NMSL   Southwest Room, New Mexico State Library, Santa Fe.

OSA   Oregon State Library Correspondence, RGL8, Oregon State Archives, Salem.

OSU   Oregon State University Library Correspondence, RG9, Microfilm Reels, Oregon State University Archives, Corvallis.

RAF   Riverside Alumni File [School of Library Service], Special Collections Department, Riverside City and County Public Library, Riverside, California.

SWM   Southwest Museum, Los Angeles, California.

TANM   Territorial Archives of New Mexico, Microfilm Edition, 72–1180–1181, New Mexico State Archives, Santa Fe.

UAZ   University of Arizona Archives, Tucson, Arizona.

UID   University of Idaho, Melvin A. Brannon Correspondence, Special Collections Department, Moscow, Idaho.

UOR   University of Oregon, Library Correspondence, University Archives, Eugene, Oregon.

UWA   University of Washington, Library Director's Office Records, RG 73–22, University Archives, Seattle, Washington.

UWM   University of Wisconsin-Madison, Archives, Madison, Wisconsin.

WFLC   Wisconsin Free Library Commission, Series 1076, State Historical Society of Wisconsin, Madison.

WLSP   Wisconsin Library School Placement Files, University
       Archives, University of Wisconsin-Madison.
WSL   Washington State Library, General Correspondence,
       Washington State Archives, Olympia.

Introduction, pp. xiii–xix

1. For discussions of the West's masculine image see, for example, Richard White, *"It's Your Misfortune and None of My Own": A History of the American West* (Norman: University of Oklahoma Press, 1991), 627; and Katherine G. Morrissey, "Engendering the West," in *Under an Open Sky: Rethinking America's Western Past,* eds. William Cronon, George Miles, and Jay Gitlin (New York: W. W. Norton and Company, 1992), 133.

2. Early library school classes tended to be racially homogeneous. The first African-American woman did not graduate from library school until 1923. For studies that address our multicultural western heritage see, for example, Susan Armitage, "Through Women's Eyes: A New View of the West," in *The Women's West,* eds. Susan Armitage and Elizabeth Jameson (Norman: University of Oklahoma Press, 1987), 9–18; Lawrence B. de Graaf, "Race, Sex, and Region: Black Women in the American West, 1850–1920," *Pacific Historical Review* 49 (May 1980): 285–313; Sarah Deutsch, *No Separate Refuge: Culture, Class, and Gender on an Anglo-Hispanic Frontier in the American Southwest, 1880–1940* (New York: Oxford University Press, 1987); Elizabeth Jameson, "Towards a Multicultural History of Women in the Western United States," *Signs: Journal of Women in Culture and Society* 13 (Summer 1988): 761–91; Patricia Nelson Limerick, *The Legacy of Conquest: The Unbroken Past of the American West* (New York: W. W. Norton, 1987); Peggy Pascoe, "Western Women at the Cultural Crossroads," in *Trails: Toward a New Western History,* eds. Patricia Nelson Limerick, Clyde A. Milner II, and Charles E. Rankin (Lawrence: University Press of Kansas, 1991), 40–58; and Lillian Schlissel, Vicki L. Ruiz, and Janice Monk, eds., *Western Women, Their Land, Their Lives* (Albuquerque: University of New Mexico Press, 1988).

3. LeeAnne G. Kryder, "Self-Assertion and Social Commitment: The Significance of Work to the Progressive Era's New Woman," *Journal of American Culture* 6 (Summer 1983): 25–30.

4. Wayne A. Wiegand, *"An Active Instrument for Propaganda": The*

American Public Library During World War I (New York: Greenwood Press, 1989).

5. Lynn Gordon, *Gender and Higher Education in the Progressive Era* (New Haven: Yale University Press, 1990), 10.

6. See, for example, Paula M. Bauman, "Single Women Homesteaders in Wyoming, 1880–1930," *Annals of Wyoming* 58 (Spring 1986): 39–49; Sarah M. Nelson, "Widowhood and Autonomy in the Native-American Southwest," 22–41, and Joyce D. Goodfriend, "The Struggle for Survival: Widows in Denver, 1880–1912," 166–94, in *On Their Own: Widows and Widowhood in the American Southwest, 1848–1939,* ed. Arlene Scadron (Urbana: University of Illinois Press, 1988); Lesley Poling-Kemp, *The Harvey Girls: Women Who Opened the West* (New York: Paragon House, 1989); Claudia Goldin, "The Work and Wages of Single Women, 1870–1920," *Journal of Economic History* 40 (March 1980): 81–88. For studies of prostitution, see Anne M. Butler, *Daughters of Joy, Sisters of Misery: Prostitutes in the American West, 1865–90* (Urbana: University of Illinois Press, 1985); Marion S. Goldman, *Gold Diggers and Silver Miners: Prostitution and Social Life on the Comstock Lode* (Ann Arbor: University of Michigan Press, 1981); and Mary Murphy, "The Private Lives of Public Women: Prostitution in Butte, Montana, 1878–1917," in *The Women's West,* eds. Armitage and Jameson, 193–205. For studies of teachers and college professors, see Kathleen Underwood, "The Pace of Their Own Lives: Teacher Training and the Life Course of Western Women," *Pacific Historical Review* 55 (November 1986): 513–30; Mary Hurblert Cordier, *Schoolwomen of the Prairies and Plains: Personal Narratives from Iowa, Kansas, and Nebraska, 1860s–1920s* (Albuquerque: University of New Mexico Press, 1992); and Geraldine Joncich Clifford, ed., *The Lone Voyagers: Academic Women in Coeducational Institutions, 1870–1937* (New York: The Feminist Press, 1989).

7. Joanne Meyerowitz, *Women Adrift: Independent Wage Earners in Chicago, 1880–1930* (Chicago: University of Chicago Press, 1988); and Kathy Peiss, *Cheap Amusements: Working Women and Leisure in Turn-of-the-Century New York* (Philadelphia: Temple University Press, 1986).

8. For a study of western community building, see Kathleen Underwood, *Town Building on the Colorado Frontier* (Albuquerque: University of New Mexico Press, 1987). For additional information about

women's clubs, see Jane C. Croly, *The History of the Women's Club Movement in America* (New York: Henry G. Allen & Co., 1898); Theodora Penny Martin, *The Sound of Our Own Voices: Women's Study Clubs, 1860–1910* (Boston: Beacon Press, 1987); and Anne Firor Scott, *Natural Allies: Women's Associations in American History* (Urbana: University of Illinois Press, 1991).

9. Suzanne Hildenbrand, "A Historical Perspective on Gender Issues in American Librarianship," *The Canadian Journal of Information Science* 17 (September 1992): 18–28. For further discussion of the absence of women from American library history, see also Laurel A. Grotzinger, "Biographical Research on Women Librarians: Its Paucity, Perils and Pleasures," in *The Status of Women in Librarianship: Historical, Sociological and Economic Issues,* ed. Kathleen Heim (New York: Neal-Schuman, 1983), 139–90; and Mary Niles Maack, "Towards a History of Women in Librarianship: A Critical Analysis with Suggestions for Further Research," *Journal of Library History* 17 (Spring 1982): 164–85.

10. Dee Garrison, *Apostles of Culture: The Public Librarian and American Society, 1876–1920* (New York: Free Press, 1979).

11. Hildenbrand, "A Historical Perspective on Gender Issues," 25.

12. Sources consulted include *Library Journal,* 1887–1917; *Public Libraries,* 1896–1917; *New York State Library School Register, 1887–1926* (Albany: New York State Library School Association, 1959); Graduates' Association of the Pratt Institute Library School, *Report for the Year Ending March 8, 1901: Constitution and List of Members* (New York: Evening Post Job Printing House, 1901); Library School of the University of Wisconsin, *Directory of Graduates for Twenty-five Classes, 1907–1931* (Madison: The School, 1931); University of Washington Alumni Association, *Register of Graduates, 1913–1940* (Seattle: University of Washington School of Librarianship, 1940); *Library School Register of Graduates, 1893–1957* (Philadelphia: Drexel Institute of Technology, 1958); and *Who's Who in Library Service* (New York: The Grolier Society, 1933).

13. Sarah K. Vann, *Training for Librarianship Before 1923* (Chicago: American Library Association, 1961).

14. A University of Washington register of graduates, prepared in 1925, shows seven employed in California, one in Colorado, four in Idaho, seventeen in Oregon, and ninety-two in Washington.

1. Mabel Newcomer, *A Century of Higher Education for American Women* (New York: Harper, 1959), 56.

2. See, for example, Richard M. Bernard and Maris Vinovskis, "The Female School Teacher in Ante-Bellum Massachusetts," *Journal of Social History* 10 (1977): 332–45; Rosalind Rosenberg, *Divided Lives: American Women in the Twentieth Century* (New York: Hill and Wang, 1992); and Kathleen Underwood, "The Pace of Their Own Lives: Teacher Training and the Life Course of Western Women," *Pacific Historical Review* 55 (November 1986): 513–30.

3. Mary E. Ahern, "The Business Side of a Woman's Career as a Librarian," *Library Journal* 24 (July 1899): 60–62.

4. Herbert Putnam, "What it Means to be a Librarian," *Ladies' Home Journal* 17 (February 1900): 22; and Mary E. Hazeltine to Robert P. Bliss, 4 October 1906, WFLC, Box 1.

5. See, in particular, Andrew D. Abbott, *The System of Professions: An Essay on the Division of Expert Labor* (Chicago: University of Chicago Press, 1988); Magali Sarfatti Larson, *The Rise of Professionalism: A Sociological Analysis* (Berkeley: University of California Press, 1977); and Samuel Haber, *The Quest for Authority and Honor in the American Professions, 1750–1900* (Chicago: University of Chicago Press, 1991).

6. *Public Libraries* 14 (January 1909): 16; Minutes of the Faculty, Wisconsin Library School, 4 May 1910, UWA; and Carl M. White, *A Historical Introduction to Library Education: Problems and Progress to 1951* (Metuchen, NJ: Scarecrow Press, 1976), 255.

7. Valmai R. Fenster, "The University of Wisconsin Library School, A History, 1895–1921" (Ph.D. diss., University of Wisconsin-Madison, 1977); George F. Bowerman, "Libraries," in *International Yearbook: A Compendium of the World's Progress, 1900* (New York: Dodd, 1901); and White, *A Historical Introduction to Library Education.*

8. See, for example, Julie Roy Jeffrey, *Frontier Women: The Trans-Mississippi West, 1840–1888* (New York: Hill and Wang, 1979). For a historiographical review of the literature of frontier women, see Glenda Riley, "Frontier Women," in *American Frontier and Western Issues: A Historiographical Review,* ed. Roger L. Nichols (New York: Greenwood Press, 1986), 179–98.

9. White, *"It's Your Misfortune,"* 277.

10. Glenda Riley, *The Female Frontier: A Comparative View of Women*

on the Prairie and the Plains (Lawrence: University Press of Kansas, 1988), 2. To achieve a well-balanced study, however, it is important to take both gender and regional influences into consideration. See Susan H. Armitage, "Gender and Regionalism," in *Regional Studies: The Interplay of Land and People,* ed. Glen E. Lich (College Station: Texas A & M University Press, 1992).

11. Elizabeth Jameson, "Women as Workers, Women as Civilizers: True Womanhood in the American West," in *The Women's West,* eds. Susan Armitage and Elizabeth Jameson (Norman: University of Oklahoma Press, 1987), 158.

12. Mary Hurlbut Cordier, *Schoolwomen of the Prairies and Plains* (Albuquerque: University of New Mexico Press, 1992), 297. See also Kathleen Underwood, "The Pace of Their Own Lives: Teacher Training and the Life Course of Western Women," *Pacific Historical Review* 55 (November 1986): 513–30; and *American Teachers: Histories of a Profession at Work,* ed. Donald R. Warren (New York: Macmillan, 1989). See Nancy Hoffman, *Woman's "True" Profession: Voices from the History of Education* (Old Westbury, NY: The Feminist Press, 1981); and Polly Welts Kaufman, *Women Teachers on the Frontier* (New Haven: Yale University Press, 1984) for accounts of teachers east of the Mississippi.

13. For example, see Mary Ellen Hanson and Carl A. Hanson, "Wilma Loy Shelton: Library Leader in New Mexico, 1920–1950," *New Mexico Historical Review* 64 (January 1989): 51–76; Gail K. Nelson and John V. Richardson, "Adelaide Hasse and the Early History of the U.S. Superintendent of Documents Classification Scheme," *Government Publications Review* 13 (January/February 1986): 79–96; Denise Sallee, "Reconceptualizing Women's History: Anne Hadden and the California County Library System," *Libraries & Culture* 27 (Fall 1992): 351–77; Virginia Scharff, "The Independent and Feminine Life: Grace Raymond Hebard, 1861–1936," in *Lone Voyagers: Academic Women in Coeducational Institutions, 1870–1937,* ed. Geraldine Joncich Clifford (New York: The Feminist Press, 1989), 127–45; and Wayne A. Wiegand, "Lion and the Lady Revisited: Another Look at the Firing of Mary L. Jones as Los Angeles Public Librarian in 1905," *Library and Information Science Research* 5 (Fall 1983): 273–90.

14. For an extended discussion, see Joan Jacobs Brumburg and Nancy Tomes, "Women in the Professions: A Research Agenda for American Historians," *Reviews in American History* 10 (June 1982): 275–96; and Penina M. Glazer and Miriam Slater, *Unequal Colleagues:*

The Entrance of Women into the Professions, 1890–1940 (New Brunswick: Rutgers University Press, 1987).

15. Nancy F. Cott, *The Grounding of Modern Feminism* (New Haven: Yale University Press, 1987), 225.

16. Barbara Miller Solomon, *In the Company of Educated Women: A History of Women and Higher Education in America* (New Haven: Yale University Press, 1985), 127.

17. Susan Porter Benson, *Counter Cultures: Saleswomen, Managers, and Customers in American Department Stores, 1890–1940* (Urbana: University of Illinois Press, 1986); and Marjorie W. Davies, *Woman's Place is at the Typewriter: Office Work and Office Workers, 1870–1930* (Philadelphia: Temple University Press, 1983).

18. Margaret W. Rossiter, *Women Scientists in America: Struggles and Strategies to 1940* (Baltimore: The Johns Hopkins University Press, 1982).

19. For an extended discussion, see Susan M. Reverby, *Ordered to Care: The Dilemma of American Nursing, 1850–1945* (New York: Cambridge University Press, 1987); and Barbara Melosh, *The Physician's Hand: Work, Culture, and Conflict in American Nursing* (Philadelphia: Temple University Press, 1982.

20. Caroline M. Hewins, "Library Work for Women," *Library Journal* 16 (September 1891): 274.

21. Typewritten note, n.d. [1906], Lummis Papers, SWM. Lummis and Missouri librarian Joseph F. Daniels appear to have associated the decline of the profession with feminization. Daniels wrote: "There are very few librarians now alive—they have been growing less in the last twenty-five years." Daniels to Charles F. Lummis, 9 March 1906, Lummis Papers, MS1, Box 1A, SWM.

22. Frederick Crunden, "Fifth Session," *Library Journal* 30 (Conference No. 1905): 170.

23. Mary E. Robbins, "Notes by a Library Organizer," *Library Journal* 28 (January 1903): 14–15.

24. Caroline V. Langworthy to Frances Simpson, 8 May 1908, Langworthy LSAF.

25. Michael P. Malone and Richard W. Etulain, *The American West: A Twentieth-century History* (Lincoln: University of Nebraska Press, 1989), 122, 155.

26. White, *"It's Your Misfortune,"* 278.

27. Charles F. Lummis to Theodore Roosevelt, 23 August 1905, Lummis Papers, M1PL5, SWM.

28. Haynes McMullen, "The Prevalence of Libraries in the Middle West and Far West Before 1876," *Libraries & Culture* 26 (Spring 1991): 441–63; and John Cotton Dana, "The Library Movement in the Far West," *The Library* 8 (1896): 446–50.

29. Mabel Shrum to Katharine L. Sharp, 9 September 1900, Shrum LSAF; and Charles W. Smith, "Library Conditions in the Northwest," *Library Journal* 30 (1905): 12.

30. W. P. Kimball, "The Library Situation in California," *Library Journal* 27 (1902): 200–201; Dana, "The Library Movement in the Far West," 447; Ida A. Kidder to Katharine L. Sharp, [February 1907], Kidder LSAF; and Mary E. Hazeltine to Doris Greene, 7 April 1919, Greene LSSR.

31. Jane C. Croly, *The History of the Women's Club Movement in America* (New York: Henry G. Allen & Co., 1898).

32. Local Club Records, Montana, GFWC; and Croly, *The History of the Women's Club Movement in America,* 370.

33. Sophonisba P. Breckinridge, *Women in the Twentieth Century* (New York: McGraw Hill, 1933), 93; and Karen J. Blair, *The Clubwoman as Feminist: True Womanhood Redefined, 1868–1914* (New York: Holmes & Meier, 1980), 119.

34. Local Club Records, Utah, Oregon, Arizona, and Montana, GFWC.

35. White, *"It's Your Misfortune,"* 182.

36. Kathleen Underwood, *Town Building on the Colorado Frontier* (Albuquerque: University of New Mexico Press, 1987), xviii.

37. Mabel E. Prentiss to J. L. Gillis, 17 March 1906, CLOF; and Mrs. A. A. Warrick to E. J. Dockery, 19 September 1902, IFLC.

38. Adele L. Nichols to Henry E. Legler, 11 February 1909, WFLC, Box 2; and Henry E. Legler to Mrs. H. D. Nichols, WFLC, Box 4.

39. Croly, *The History of the Women's Club Movement in America,* 853.

40. Caroline A. Platt, "Early History of the Alamosa Carnegie Library," 11 May 1946, Mss. M619, M46–431, DPLA.

41. Bertha Kumli to J. L. Gillis, 22 November 1905 and 15 December 1905, CLOF.

42. These range from California in 1872 to Utah in 1896.

43. James Bertram to Gertrude Buckhous, 15 February 1916, Fort Benton, Montana CLC, Reel 10; and Mabel E. Prentiss to J. L. Gillis, 7 December 1905, CLOF.

44. Charles Wesley Smith, "Library Conditions in the Northwest," *Library Journal* 30 (Conference No. 1905): 10–13.

Chapter 2, pp. 17–39

Epigraph: Katharine L. Sharp to Cornelia Marvin, 26 June 1906, OSA, Box 12.

1. Robert M. Crunden, *Ministers of Reform: The Progressives' Achievement in American Civilization, 1889–1920* (Urbana: University of Illinois, 1984), ix, 275; and Albert Hardy to Katharine L. Sharp, 15 January 1896, KLS, Box 2.

2. John Edward Van Male, "A History of Library Extension in Colorado, 1890–1930" (M.A. thesis, University of Denver, 1940), 21.

3. Viola H. Schell to Phineas L. Windsor, 26 June 1916, Clara Abernethy LSAF; Josephine Rathbone to Cornelia Marvin, 13 March 1913, OSA, Box 12; Lucy L. Pleasants to Mary E. Hazeltine, 6 March 1916, Emily Richie LSSR; and Hazeltine to Marvin, 29 May 1913, OSA, Box 2.

4. Barbara Sicherman, "Sense and Sensibility: A Case Study of Women's Reading in Late-Victorian America," in *Reading in America: Literature and Social History*, ed. Cathy Davidson (Baltimore: Johns Hopkins University Press, 1989), 202; Theodora Penny Martin, *The Sound of Our Own Voices: Women's Study Clubs, 1860– 1910* (Boston: Beacon Press, 1987); and Barbara Sicherman, "Reading and Ambition: M. Carey Thomas and Female Heroism," *American Quarterly* 45 (March 1993): 73–103.

5. A number of library schools asked students to comment on the nature and extent of their reading when they applied for admission.

6. Valmai R. Fenster, "The University of Wisconsin Library School, A History, 1895–1921" (Ph.D. diss., University of Wisconsin-Madison, 1977), 174.

7. Joseph F. Daniels to Frances D. Patterson, 16 February 1917, Julia Clapperton RAF.

8. Camille Wallace to Charlotte A. Baker, 10 March 1912, CAB.

9. Mary E. Hazeltine to J. M. Hitt, 1 August 1913, WSL, Box 19.

10. Data are not complete for the women's ages at the time of graduation from library school, but based on the number of years that elapsed between college and receipt of the library school certificate, the average age would have been approximately twenty-seven.

11. William E. Henry to Mary E. Hazeltine, 14 February 1911, WLSP; Edna Sanderson to Frances Simpson, 22 May 1912, Lily Gray LSAF; and Minutes of the Denver Public Library Commission, 11 May 1907, DPLA.

12. Mabel Powell to Harry Coffman, 19 June 1901, UWA, Box 1; and Ardella B. Calkins to Joseph F. Daniels, 9 March 1916, Calkins RAF.

13. Nelle C. Bartlett, 1917 Library School Application, Bartlett RAF; and Mary Royce Crawford, 1914 Library School Application, Crawford RAF.

14. Mabel Chase Grover to Joseph F. Daniels, 31 July 1915, Grover RAF; and Mabel Anderson to Daniels, 3 August 1919, Anderson RAF.

15. Grace Raymond Hebard to William C. Deming, [1930], "Library Portrait Recalls Former History Professor," *Branding Iron* 10 (February 1932), GRH, Box 6, and Grace Raymond Hebard to Aven Nelson, 11 February 1928, GRH.

16. Katharine L. Sharp to Alice Tyler, 10 March 1905, Della A. Northey LSAF.

17. Ida A. Kidder to William B. Ayer, 13 June 1919, OSU, Reel 9.

18. Ida A. Kidder to Elizabeth Forrest, 17 January 1916, OSU, Reel 3.

19. Agnes Dickerson to Mary E. Hazeltine, March 1917, Dickerson LSSR.

20. Katharine L. Sharp to William E. Henry, 1 June 1905, ISLC; Mary Wright Plummer to Cornelia Marvin, 19 January 1909, OSA, Box 2; James I. Wyer to Matthew H. Douglass, 11 September 1908, UOR; and Albert S. Wilson to Mary Frances Isom, 27 November 1908, Myrtle Knepper LSAF.

21. Everett L. Perry to Mary E. Hazeltine, 5 September 1918, WLSP.

22. Mary Wright Plummer to Cornelia Marvin, 27 November 1905, OSA, Box 2.

23. Charles C. Williamson, *Training for Library Work*, reprinted in *The Williamson Reports of 1921 and 1923* (Metuchen, NJ: Scarecrow Press, 1971).

24. "Old Maid's Paradise," GRH.

25. Winnie Bucklin to Mary E. Hazeltine, 7 November 1910, Bucklin LSSR; and Roxana G. Johnson to Frances Simpson, 20 June 1917, LSAF.

26. James I. Wyer, Jr., to Cornelia Marvin, 16 September 1912, OSA, Box 15; and Charlotte A. Baker to H. Richie, 19 May 1912, Baker to Elizabeth McNeal, 22 August 1914, and Baker to Mabel Shrum Tilley, 4 October 1913, CAB.

27. Pansy L. Bolton Rennie to Joseph F. Daniels, 16 November 1916, Bolton RAF.

28. Anne D. Swezey to Phineas L. Windsor, 18 January 1917, Swezey LSAF; Mrs. Jessie Hoyt-Hatch to Bertha Kumli, 15 October 1908, CLOF; and Mary E. Hazeltine to Mary F. Sheriff, 17 April 1913, Agnes Dickerson LSSR.

29. Katharine L. Sharp to Mary Wright Plummer, 28 May 1904, LSDL; and Mary Frances Isom to Cornelia Marvin, 22 September 1911, OSA, Box 17.

30. Lutie Stearns to Cornelia Marvin, 11 July 1911, OSA, Box 23; and Charlotte A. Baker to "Papa" Parsons, 25 September 1914, CAB. Although the letter from Stearns to Marvin survived, additional information about Marvin's "little girl" has not.

31. Joyce Antler, " 'After College, What?': New Graduates and the Family Claim," *American Quarterly* 32 (Fall 1980): 412, 433.

32. Willia K. Garver to Katharine L. Sharp, 15 January 1907, Garver LSAF; Irene Warren to Sharp, 30 October 1896, KLS, Box 1; and Mayme Batterson to Anna Price, [1910], Batterson LSAF.

33. Edna Goss to Katharine L. Sharp, 14 September 1903, Goss LSAF.

34. Lena Brownell to Mary E. Hazeltine, 30 July 1912, Brownell LSSR.

35. Mayme Batterson to Albert S. Wilson, 8 February 1909, Batterson LSAF.

36. Mayme Batterson to Albert S. Wilson, 21 January 1909, Batterson LSAF; Mabel G. West to Frances Simpson, 28 January 1914, OSA, Box 17; and Mary E. Smith to Simpson, 27 June 1919, Smith LSAF.

37. M. Hale Douglass to Cornelia Marvin, 4 February 1909, OSA, Box 22; and Lena Brownell to Mary E. Hazeltine, 30 July 1912, Brownell LSSR.

38. Frances Simpson to Mabel M. Reynolds, 26 April 1906, Reynolds LSAF.

39. William E. Henry to Mary E. Hazeltine, 26 June 1917, WLSP.

40. Flora B. Roberts to Mary E. Hazeltine, 16 December 1912, Brownell LSSR.

41. Margaret Dunbar to Cornelia Marvin, 29 October 1911, OSA, Box 2.

42. Willia K. Garver to Cornelia Marvin, 12 March 1917, OSA, Box 2.

43. Mabel F. Barnum, "Opportunities for College Women in the Library Profession," *Bostonia* 14 (April 1913): 6; and Ella F. Corwin to William E. Henry, 30 July 1909, OSA, Box 1.

44. Edna D. Bullock to J. M. Hitt, 14 December 1905; and Helen Calhoun to J. M. Hitt, 9 August 1907, WSL, Box 19; and Agnes Cole to Phineas L. Windsor, 1 September 1916, Cole LSAF.

45. Mary E. Hazeltine to Matt Murray, April 1917, WLSP.

46. Grace L. Yerington to J. M. Hitt, 28 June 1910, WSL, Box 19; Mary E. Hazeltine to Judson T. Jennings, 3 June 1912, WLSP; and Katherine Kiemle to Hazeltine, 20 January 1912, Kiemle LSSR.

47. Mabel Shrum to Katharine L. Sharp, 9 September 1900, Shrum LSAF; and Margaret Sweet to James F. Ailshie, 27 January 1904, JFA.

Chapter 3, pp. 41–58

Epigraph: Lucy M. Lewis to Katharine L. Sharp, 4 November 1906, Lewis LSAF.

1. Belle Sweet Oral History, MBS; and Mary E. Downey, "Pioneering in Utah," *Bulletin of the American Library Association* 9 (1915): 143.

2. Florence Farnham to Mary E. Hazeltine, 14 March 1910, Farnham LSSR; Belle Sweet to Class of 1904, 28 February 1907, Sweet LSAF; and Roxana G. Johnson to Frances Simpson, 18 June 1910, Johnson LSAF.

3. "Charlotte A. Baker," *New York State College Alumni Quarterly* 17 (Spring 1936): n.p.; and Lucy M. Lewis to Katharine L. Sharp, 4 November 1906, Lewis LSAF.

4. Maud R. MacPherson to Henry E. Legler, 20 April 1909, WFLC, Box 4; *Annual Catalogue of the Officers and Students of the State Normal School, Cheney, Washington, 1895–96* (Olympia, Washington: O. C. White, 1896), 9; Jane Schauers to Mary E. Hazeltine, 14 September 1908, Schauers LSSR; Ruth E. Wright to Carl H. Milam, 2 May 1910, OSA, Box 11.

5. Roxana G. Johnson to Frances Simpson, 14 June 1910, 18 June 1910, Johnson LSAF.

6. Sweet Oral History, MBS; Roxana G. Johnson to Frances Simpson, 18 June 1910, Johnson LSAF.

7. Lena Brownell to Mary E. Hazeltine, 27 April 1913, Brownell LSSR; Lucy M. Lewis to Katharine L. Sharp, 4 November 1906, and Lewis to Phineas L. Windsor, 26 January 1910, Lewis LSAF.

8. Sweet Oral History, MBS; and Elizabeth Stout to Frances Simpson, 19 April 1909, Stout LSAF.

9. Estelle Lutrell, "History of the University of Arizona, 1885–1926," 112, Unpublished manuscript, Estelle Lutrell Papers, UAZ.

10. Lucy M. Lewis to Katharine L. Sharp, 4 November 1906, Lewis LSAF.

11. Sweet Oral History, MBS.

12. Mabel Prentiss to J. L. Gillis, 10 December 1905, CLOF.

13. Mabel Wilkinson, "Development of the Platte County Free Library, February to June 1915," Wyoming State Historical Research and Publications Division, Cheyenne; and Bertha Kumli to J. L. Gillis, 3 December 1905, CLOF.

14. Librarian's Report, 1 September 1910, MCPL; Sweet Oral History, MBS; and Mary Hubbard to Frances Simpson, 21 September [1913], Hubbard LSAF.

15. Sweet Oral History, MBS; and Mary Frances Isom to Cornelia Marvin, 1 October 1915, OSA, Box 4.

16. Belle Sweet to Mary N. Roberts, 3 September 1908, Sweet Letterpress, MBS; M. Hale Douglass to Beatrice J. Barker, 19 October 1908, UOR; Ethel A. Hickey to Wisconsin Library School, 24 October 1910, WLSP; and Elizabeth Stout to Albert S. Wilson, 10 April 1909, Stout LSAF.

17. Cornelia Marvin to Mirpah Blair, 23 May 1913, OSA, Box 4; and Charlotte A. Baker to John M. Scott, 7 November 1912, CAB.

18. Winnie Bucklin to Mary E. Hazeltine, 23 February 1914, Bucklin LSSR; Roxana G. Johnson to Frances Simpson, 20 June 1917, Johnson LSAF; Fenimore Schwartz to Simpson, 8 June 1916, Schwartz LSAF; and Lily Grey to Katharine L. Sharp, 27 March 1907, Grey LSAF.

19. Reba Davis to Frances Simpson, 4 January 1917, Davis LSAF; and Agnes Mathilde Wergeland file, GRH.

20. Roxana G. Johnson to Cornelia Marvin, 14 March 1911, OSA, Box 1.

21. Luther Foster to Lucy M. Lewis, 1 August 1906, Lewis to Katharine L. Sharp, 4 November 1906, Lewis LSAF; Charlotte A. Baker to R. H. Corwin, 12 December 1911, CAB; and *Gem of the Mountains* [University of Idaho Annual], 1906 (Columbus, Idaho: The Champlin Press, 1906), 29.

22. Ida A. Kidder to Lucy M. Lewis, 15 March 1911, OSU, Reel 31.

23. Belle Sweet to Class of 1904, 28 February 1907, Sweet LSAF.

24. Belle Sweet to Ida Wolf, 7 June 1913, Letterpress, MBS.

25. Belle Sweet to A. M. Akin, 11 May 1910, Letterpress, MBS; Sweet to Katharine L. Sharp, 28 February 1907, Sweet LSAF; and Mayme Batterson to Phineas L. Windsor, 11 April 1910, Batterson LSAF.

26. *Gem of the Mountains 1907* (Columbus, Idaho: The Champlin Press, 1907), 22; and Belle Sweet to A. M. Akin, 11 May 1910, Sweet Letterpress, MBS.

27. Mabel Prentiss to J. L. Gillis, 12 December 1905, CLOF; and Mabel Wilkinson, "Development of the Platte County Free Library."

28. Theodora Brewitt to Mary E. Hazeltine, 17 March [1911 or 1912], Brewitt LSSR; Florence Farnham to Hazeltine, 14 March 1910, Farnham LSSR; and Dorothy Ely to Hazeltine, 3 August 1915, Ely LSSR.

29. Edith Morgan to Frances Simpson, 17 October 1916, Morgan LSAF.

30. Lucy M. Lewis to Katharine L. Sharp, 4 November 1906, Lewis LSAF; and Charlotte A. Baker to Lewis, 8 March 1909, and Baker to H. Richie, 5 November 1912, CAB.

31. Mary E. Petty, "Trailblazing Librarians: The Women Who Founded the Spokane Mountaineers," *ALKI: The Washington Library Association Journal* 8 (December 1992): 23–25.

32. Katharine L. Sharp to Lucy M. Lewis, 12 November 1906, LSDL; Sharp to Lily Gray, 2 April 1907, Gray LSAF; Lewis to Sharp, 4 November 1906, Lewis LSAF; Gray to Sharp, 8 March 1907, Gray LSAF; and Ida A. Kidder to Sharp, February 1907, Kidder LSAF.

33. Corine Kittelson to Mary E. Hazeltine, 12 August 1913, Kittelson LSSR.

34. Katharine L. Sharp to Ida A. Kidder, 19 February 1907, Kidder LSAF.

35. Ida A. Kidder to Katharine L. Sharp, 30 July 1906, Kidder LSAF; and Lavina Stewart to Mary E. Hazeltine, 13 April 1918, Stewart LSSR.

36. Agnes Dickerson to Mary E. Hazeltine, 15 March 1914, Dickerson LSSR; and Corine Kittelson to Hazeltine, 29 November 1912, Kittelson LSSR.

37. Albert S. Wilson to Roxana G. Johnson, 24 June 1910, Johnson LSSR; Mary E. Hazeltine to Dorothy B. Ely, 24 August 1915, Ely LSSR; and Wilson to Mayme Batterson, 25 June 1909, Batterson LSAF.

38. Lena Brownell to Mary E. Hazeltine, 27 April 1913, Brownell LSSR.

39. Lula Smith to Cornelia Marvin, 25 September 1914, OSA, Box 3.

40. Mary Frances Isom to Cornelia Marvin, 21 December 1914, OSA, Box 17; and Ida A. Kidder to Marvin, 7 May 1919, OSU, Reel 9.

41. Theodora Brewitt to Mary E. Hazeltine, 12 August [1911 or 1912], Brewitt LSSR; Althea Warren to Mary E. Hazeltine, 5 April 1916, WLSP; and Julia C. Stockett to M. A. Brannon, 1 June 1916, UID.

42. Mary E. Hazeltine to Harriet Kidder, 29 February 1916, Kidder LSSR.

43. Edna Goss to Katharine L. Sharp, 14 September 1903, Goss LSAF; and Lucy M. Lewis to Phineas L. Windsor, 11 September 1920, Lewis LSAF.

44. Jane Schauers to Mary E. Hazeltine, 12 October 1908, Schauers LSSR; Elizabeth Ritchie to A. S. Wilson, 21 May 1912, Ritchie LSAF; and Edith Morgan to Frances Simpson, 17 October 1916, Morgan LSAF.

Chapter 4, pp. 59–77

Epigraph: C. A. Duniway to Phineas L. Windsor, 9 April 1913, Flora M. Case LSAF.

1. The years from 1900 to 1920 represent a period of burgeoning land-grant colleges and a time when principal opportunities for women who wished to become college educators shifted to the land-grant colleges. For a more extensive discussion, see Jesse Bernard, *Academic Women* (University Park: Pennsylvania State University Press, 1964), and Rosalind Rosenberg, "The Limits of Access: The History of Coeducation in America," in *Women and Higher Education in American*

History, eds. John Mack Faragher and Florence Howe (New York: W. W. Norton, 1988), 107–29.

2. Elizabeth T. Stout to Frances Simpson, 10 November 1916, Stout LSAF; and Belle Sweet to Katharine L. Sharp, 7 November 1905.

3. Edith Morgan to Phineas L. Windsor, 17 July 1917, Morgan LSAF; and Charlotte A. Baker to Lucy M. Lewis, 8 March 1909, CAB.

4. Josephine Meissner to Katharine L. Sharp, 11 November 1906, Meissner LSAF.

5. Fenimore Schwartz to Frances Simpson, 22 June 1914, LSAF.

6. Charlotte A. Baker to Lucy M. Lewis, 8 March 1909, CAB.

7. Belle Sweet to Katharine L. Sharp, 27 January 1906, Sweet LSAF; and Elizabeth Forrest to Frances Simpson, 21 January 1915, Forrest LSAF.

8. Mabel Reynolds to Katharine L. Sharp, 26 March 1907, Reynolds LSAF; and Lucy M. Lewis to Frances Simpson, 28 March 1908, Lewis LSAF.

9. Mabel M. Reynolds to Katharine L. Sharp, 3 June 1904, Reynolds LSAF; Roxana G. Johnson to Frances Simpson and Albert S. Wilson, 14 June 1910, Johnson LSAF; and Katharine Kiemle to Mary E. Hazeltine, 19 October 1910, Kiemle LSSR.

10. Belle Sweet to Edna Goss, 9 April 1915, Letterpress, MBS; and Julia Stockett to Mary E. Hazeltine, 4 November 1916, Stockett LSSR.

11. Theodora Brewitt to Mary E. Hazeltine, 17 March [1911 or 1912], Brewitt LSSR; and Lucy M. Lewis to Frances Simpson, 21 August 1908, Lewis LSAF.

12. Lucy M. Lewis to Katharine L. Sharp, 6 September 1906, Lewis LSAF.

13. Charlotte A. Baker to Lucy M. Lewis, 8 March 1909, CAB; Lewis to Katharine L. Sharp, 4 November 1906, Lewis LSAF; and Doris Greene to Mary E. Hazeltine, 10 December 1918, Greene LSSR.

14. C. M. Light, "A Forceful Defence of the Educational Institutions of the Territory," TANM, Reel 72, Frame 1521; and Lucy M. Lewis to Katharine L. Sharp, 4 November 1906, Lewis LSAF.

15. J. M. Hamilton to Frances Simpson, 20 April 1917, Stout LSAF; Elizabeth Forrest to Ida A. Kidder, 11 January 1915, OSU, Reel 3; and Myrtle Knepper to Albert S. Wilson, 18 June 1910, Knepper LSAF.

16. Lucy M. Lewis to Frances Simpson, 21 August 1908, Lewis LSAF; and Gertrude Buckhous to J. M. Hitt, 7 March 1906, WSL, Box 19.

17. David Kaser, "19th-century Academic Library Buildings," *College & Research Libraries News* 48 (September 1987): 476–78; and Ida A. Kidder to Cornelia Marvin, 17 June 1919, OSU, Reel 9.

18. Mabel Shrum to Katharine L. Sharp, 12 March 1902, Shrum LSAF; and Belle Sweet to Sharp, 27 January 1906, Sweet LSAF.

19. Belle Sweet to Katharine L. Sharp, 27 January 1906, Sweet LSAF.

20. Elizabeth Forrest to Frances Simpson, 21 January 1915, Forrest LSAF.

21. Roxana G. Johnson to Frances Simpson and Albert S. Wilson, 14 June 1910, Johnson LSAF.

22. Harriet L. Kidder to Mary E. Hazeltine, 22 February 1916, Kidder LSSR; and Elizabeth Forrest to Frances Simpson, 19 November 1914, Forrest LSAF.

23. Elizabeth Forrest to Simpson, 29 March 1916, Forrest LSAF.

24. Frances Simpson to Elizabeth Forrest, 8 December 1914, Forrest LSAF.

25. Grace Raymond Hebard, Annual Report to the President, 18 April 1914, 24 April 1916, GRH; and Charlotte A. Baker to Helen Ingersoll, 17 January 1916, CAB.

26. Belle Sweet to Frances Simpson, 2 April 1906, Sweet LSAF.

27. Belle Sweet to Frances Simpson, 19 April 1906; and Sweet to Class of 1904, 28 February 1907, Sweet LSAF.

28. Harriette Miles to Katharine L. Sharp, 25 March 1905, Miles LSAF; and Mabel H. Reynolds to Mary E. Hazeltine, 10 February 1910, WLSP.

29. Belle Sweet to Katharine L. Sharp, 27 January 1906, Sweet LSAF.

30. "Librarian's Annual Report," Colorado State Agricultural College, 1902, 1909, CAB; and Grace R. Hebard to President, University of Wyoming, 24 April 1916, GRH.

31. Ida A. Kidder to William J. Kerr, 9 May 1911; Grace Raymond Hebard to Kidder, 12 April 1916; and Elizabeth Forrest to Kidder, 10 April 1916, OSU, Reel 31.

32. Edith Morgan to Frances Simpson, 17 October 1916, Morgan LSAF.

33. Edith Morgan to Frances Simpson, 17 October 1916, Morgan LSAF; M. Hale Douglass to Cornelia Marvin, 3 December 1910, UOR;

and Julia Stockett to Mary E. Hazeltine, 4 November 1916, Stockett LSSR.

34. Beatrice J. Barker to Cornelia Marvin, 6 March 1912, OSA, Box 22.

35. Alice B. Anderson Dillon to Phineas L. Windsor, 13 July 1917, Morgan LSAF.

36. Ida A. Kidder to Cornelia Marvin, 13 April 1916, OSU, Reel 9.

37. Ida A. Kidder to Cornelia Marvin, 6 March 1916, OSU, Reel 9.

38. Ida A. Kidder to Cornelia Marvin, 14 March 1918, OSU, Reel 9.

39. Annual Report of the Librarian to the president, University of Wyoming, 12 April 1912, GRH; and Mary E. Smith to Frances Simpson, 15 July 1917, Smith LSAF.

40. Theodora Brewitt to Mary E. Hazeltine, 5 October 1911, Brewitt LSSR.

41. Theodora Brewitt to Mary E. Hazeltine, 17 March [1911 or 1912] Brewitt LSSR.

42. Belle Sweet to June R. Donnelly, 9 November 1910, Sweet Letterpress, MBS; and Edith M. Morgan to Florence Curtis, 23 September 1914, Morgan LSAF.

Chapter 5, pp. 79–101

Epigraph: Mary E. Hazeltine to Maud R. MacPherson, 22 May 1909, WFLC, Box 4.

1. Ernest C. Richardson, "Modern Library Work: Its Aims and Its Achievements," *The Dial* 38 (1 February 1905): 75.

2. Mary Frances Isom Oral History, OHS.

3. Cornelia Marvin to Mary Frances Isom, 23 April 1905, and Isom to Marvin, 28 April 1905 and 5 May 1905, OSA, Box 17. Marvin, who earned $1,800 in Wisconsin, "with promise of increase," accepted $1,200 per annum in Oregon.

4. Katharine L. Sharp, "Librarianship as a Profession," *Public Libraries* 3 (January 1898): 7.

5. Mary E. Ahern to Melvil Dewey, 10 March 1903, MDPC, Box 30.

6. Katharine L. Sharp to Cornelia Marvin, 11 November 1905,

LSDL, Box 5; and Mary E. Hazeltine to Lena Brownell, 13 September 1912, Brownell LSSR.

7. "Utah Library Gymnasium Commission," *Library Journal* 35 (April 1910): 166–67; and J. M. Hitt to Cornelia Marvin, 25 July 1905, OSA, Box 22.

8. Jessie M. Good, "The Traveling Library as a Civilizing Force," *Chautauquan* 36 (October 1902): 65–6; and Melvil Dewey, "Field and Future of Traveling Libraries," in *Traveling Libraries,* Bulletin 40 (Albany: New York State Library Home Education Department, 1901), 4, 6–9.

9. *Seventh Biennial Report of the Idaho State Library Commission for the Years 1913–14* (Weiser, Idaho: Weiser Signal, [1914]), 20.

10. Ibid.

11. Mary Grenning Mitchell to H. E. Legler, 12 August 1904, WFLC, Box 1.

12. Eliza Kerchival to E. J. Dockery, 11 November 1902, IFLC; Ella H. Perky to E. J. Dockery, 21 January 1903, IFLC; and Helen E. Haines, "The Growth of Traveling Libraries," *World's Work* 8 (September 1904): 5233.

13. *Seventh Biennial Report of the Idaho State Library Commission;* and Mabel Prentiss to J. L. Gillis, 20 May 1906, CLOF.

14. Edna Bullock to E. J. Dockery, 18 January 1903, IFLC.

15. Mrs. D. W. Rhodes to Cornelia Marvin, 14 January 1914, OSA, Box 4; *Second Biennial Report of the Oregon Library Commission, 1909* (Salem: Willis S. Duniway, 1909), 8; and *Sixth Biennial Report, Washington State Traveling Library, 1917–18* (Olympia: Frank M. Lamborn, 1919), 38.

16. *Fourth Biennial Report, Washington State Traveling Library, 1913–14* (Olympia: Frank M. Lamborn, 1914), 11, 14.

17. Nelly Fox to Cornelia Marvin, 25 February 1907, OSA, Box 17; Sarah Askew, "Library Work in the Open Country," *Annals of the American Academy of Political and Social Science* 67 (1916), 264; and *Fourth Biennial Report, Washington State Traveling Library, 1913–14* (Olympia: Frank M. Lamborn, 1914), 15.

18. Melvil Dewey Circular Letter, 16 November 1905, NSLC; and Cornelia Marvin to Matthew S. Dudgeon, 26 March 1912, OSA, Box 17.

19. Ida A. Kidder to Frances Simpson, 3 October 1907, Kidder LSAF.

20. Mabel Wilkinson, "Establishing Libraries Under Difficulties," *Bulletin of the ALA* 10 (1916): 161–69.

21. Prentiss resigned in December 1908. A survey taken in March 1909 listed 115 public libraries in California supported by taxation. When Prentiss visited the Reno, Nevada Public Library in 1907, she learned that Nevada had only one other public library, at Tonopah. Mabel Prentiss to J. L. Gillis, 15 September 1907, CLOF.

22. Bertha Kumli to J. L. Gillis, 13 January 1906, CLOF.

23. Joy Lichtenstein to J. L. Gillis, 3 November 1905, CLA; and Mabel Prentiss to Gillis, 7 December 1905, CLOF.

24. Mabel Wilkinson, "Development of the Platte County Free Library, February to June 1915," [typescript journal], Wyoming State Historical Research and Publications Division, Cheyenne.

25. Mabel Prentiss to J. L. Gillis, 1 December 1905, 4 February 1906, and 18 January 1906, CLOF.

26. Bertha Kumli to J. L. Gillis, 3 December 1905, CLOF; Mary Frances Isom to Cornelia Marvin, 13 June 1905, OSA, Box 17; Mabel Prentiss to J. L. Gillis, 17 December 1905, CLOF; and Kumli to Gillis, 11 December 1905, CLOF.

27. Bertha Kumli to J. L. Gillis, 24 November 1905, CLOF.

28. Bertha Kumli to J. L. Gillis, 3 December 1905 and 21 November 1905, CLOF.

29. Bertha Kumli to J. L. Gillis, 15 February 1906, and Mabel Prentiss to Gillis, 23 January 1906, CLOF.

30. Bertha Kumli to J. L. Gillis, 3 December 1905, CLOF.

31. Mary Downey, "Pioneering in Utah," *Bulletin of the American Library Association* 9 (1915): 138–39; and Bertha Kumli to J. L. Gillis, 24 November 1905, CLOF.

32. Mabel Prentiss to J. L. Gillis, 17 December 1905, CLOF.

33. Bertha Kumli to J. L. Gillis, 11 January 1906, 10 January 1906, 12 January 1906, CLOF.

34. Mrs. F. M. Gay to E. J. Dockery, 29 November 1902, IFLC; and Bertha Kumli to J. L. Gillis, 8 December 1905, CLOF.

35. J. C. Rich to E. J. Dockery, 21 March 1902, IFLC; and Mabel Prentiss to J. L. Gillis, 10 December 1905, CLOF.

36. H. Parmalee to Katharine L. Sharp, 18 November 1895, KLS, Box 1.

37. Mabel Prentiss to J. L. Gillis, 7 December 1905 and 1 December 1905; and Bertha Kumli to Gillis, 12 January 1906, CLOF.

38. Mabel Prentiss to J. L. Gillis, 9 January 1906, CLOF.

39. Bertha Kumli to Miss Steffans, 24 October 1907, CLOF.

40. Bertha Kumli to J. L. Gillis, 30 May 1908, CLOF.

41. Mabel Prentiss to J. L. Gillis, 17 December 1905, CLOF.

42. Mary Jenness, "Lighting the Library Beacon Fire in Wyoming," [1920], in Linda A. Clatworthy Biographical File, DEN.

43. Bertha Kumli to J. L. Gillis, 14 January 1908, CLOF; and J. M. Walker to J. M. Hitt, 9 July 1908, WSL, Box 19.

44. Mabel Prentiss to J. L. Gillis, 3 December 1905; and Bertha Kumli to Gillis, 18 January 1906 and 4 March 1906, CLOF.

Chapter 6, pp. 103–120

Epigraph: Margaret H. Dickey to Zana K. Miller, March 1909, SHSW, Box 3.

1. Cornelia Marvin to Alice Tyler, 4 March 1913, OSA, Box 11.

2. Viola Price Franklin to Cornelia Marvin, 31 May 1911, OSA, Box 1.

3. Mary Frances Isom to Cornelia Marvin, 11 October 1905, OSA, Box 17.

4. Mary Frances Isom to Cornelia Marvin, 9 June 1911, 24 April 1913, and 29 November 1913, OSA, Box 17.

5. J. L. Gillis to State Library Board of Trustees, 5 May 1909, CSLC; Gillis to Cornelia Marvin, 10 November 1913, OSA, Box 4; and Marvin to Mary Frances Isom, 26 November 1913, OSA, Box 17; and Gillis to Marvin, 22 November 1913, OSA, Box 4.

6. Mayme Batterson to Anna Price, 9 January 1910, Batterson LSAF; and Ethel A. Hickey to Secretary, Wisconsin Free Library Commission, 24 October 1910, WLSP.

7. William E. Henry to Mary E. Hazeltine, 11 May 1916, WLSP; Judson T. Jennings to Cornelia Marvin, 13 February 1913, and Mary Frances Isom to Marvin, 24 January 1913, OSA, Box 2.

8. Mary Jenness, "Lighting the Library Beacon Fire in Wyoming," [1920], Linda M. Clatworthy Biographical File, DEN.

9. Mayme Batterson to Anna Price, 9 January 1910, Batterson LSAF.

10. Secretary of the Ritzville Public Library Board to J. M. Hitt, 7 February 1917, WSL, Box 19.

11. Mrs. Clinton Folger to J. L. Gillis, 8 May [1913], CSL; and Mary
E. Hazeltine to Lotta Fleek, 24 October 1910, Fleek LSSR.

12. Ruth Stetson to Mary E. Hazeltine, 5 May 1916, WLSP.

13. Lotta Fleek to Mary E. Hazeltine, 27 June 1911, Fleek LSSR;
and Bertha Kumli to J. L. Gillis, 26 November 1907, CLOF.

14. Mayme Batterson to Albert S. Wilson, 4 April 1909; Batterson
to Anna Price, 9 January 1910, Batterson LSAF.

15. Camille Wallace to Charlotte A. Baker, 10 March 1912, CAB.

16. Edith Morgan to Frances Simpson, 17 October 1916, Morgan
LSAF.

17. Maud R. MacPherson to Henry E. Legler, 20 April 1909,
WFLC, Box 4.

18. Maud R. MacPherson to Henry E. Legler, 20 April 1909,
WFLC, Box 4; and Cornelia Marvin to Roxana G. Johnson, 3 September 1913, OSA, Box 2.

19. Della Northey to Frances Simpson, 16 December 1917,
Northey LSAF.

20. Maria H. Howlett, "The Traveling Library and the Country
Reader," *Wisconsin Library Bulletin* 1 (September 1905): 69.

21. Jenness, "Lighting the Library Beacon Fire."

22. Mary Frances Isom to Linda Eastman, 27 March 1902, Isom
Letterpress, MCPL; and Isom to Henry E. Legler, 30 March 1909,
WFLC, Box 4.

23. Mary Frances Isom Scrapbook, 9 December 1909; Librarian's
Report, 1 March 1910; and Isom to Laura Sikes, 18 August 1902, Isom
Letterpess, MCPL.

24. Ida A. Kidder to Katharine L. Sharp, 6 October 1906, Kidder
LSAF; and Mabel Wilkinson, "Development of Platte County Free Library," February to June 1915.

25. Librarian's Report, 1 November 1910, MCPL.

26. Julia Brown Asplund to Superintendent of Public Instruction,
New Mexico Territorial Board of Education, June 1909, TANM; and
"Library Bill Would Give New Mexico Thousands of Dollars," 16
March 1946, Clipping file ["Libraries"], NMSL.

27. Raymond Held, *The Rise of the Library in California* (Chicago:
American Library Association, 1973), 82.

28. Mayme Batterson to Anna Price, 9 January 1910, Batterson
LSAF.

29. Librarian's Report, 1 November 1911, MCPL; *Seventh Biennial*

Report, Washington State Traveling Library, 1919–20 (Olympia: Frank M. Lamborn, 1921), 12; and Librarian's Report, 1 February 1910 and 1 January 1911, MCPL.

30. Marie Houston to Mary E. Hazeltine, 27 April 1918, 17 March 1913, and 29 April 1913, Houston LSSR; and Cornelia Marvin to Mary E. Ahern, 20 June 1913, OSA, Box 4.

31. Librarian's Report, 1 March 1910, and 1 June 1910; Library Association of Portland Minutes, 5 March 1902, 6 August 1902, MCPL; Cornelia Marvin to F. Amelia Henry, 16 December 1914, OSA, Box 3; and Marvin to Mary Frances Isom, 17 December 1907, OSA, Box 17.

32. "Buying List of Recent Books Recommended by the Library Commissions of Iowa, Minnesota, Wisconsin, Idaho, Nebraska, and Delaware," NSLC, Box 11; and *Fourth Biennial Report of the Oregon Library Commission* (Salem: Willis S. Duniway, 1913), 9.

33. Mayme Batterson to Anna Price, 9 January 1910, Batterson LSAF; and Charlotte A. Baker to Mrs. Titus, 14 December 1914, CAB.

34. *Third Biennial Report of the Oregon Library Commission, 1911* (Salem: Willis S. Duniway, 1910), 8; Wayne A. Wiegand, "Oregon's Public Libraries During the First World War," *Oregon Historical Quarterly* 90 (Spring 1989): 43; and Lucy Baker to Charlotte A. Baker, 11 July 1915, CAB.

35. For more information about California's county libraries, see Harriet G. Eddy, *County Free Library Organizing in California, 1909–1918* (Berkeley: California Library Association, 1955); and Laura Steffens Suggett, *The Beginning and the End of the Best Library Service in the World* (San Francisco: Francisco Publishers, 1924).

36. Linda M. Clatworthy, "Library Survey of Colorado" (M.A. thesis, University of Denver, 1915); and Librarian's Report, 1 June 1910, MCPL.

37. James L. Gillis hired former high school principal Harriet G. Eddy as a county library organizer in 1909 to ensure the success of the library-school cooperation. Gillis to State Library Board of Trustees, 8 January 1910, CSLC; Theodora Brewitt application for a county library position, 1916, Application for County Librarian, CSLC; and undated newspaper clipping, Vera Snook LSAF.

38. Della Northey to Phineas L. Windsor, 18 November 1912, Northey LSAF; and Sarah Askew to Cornelia Marvin, 14 November 1913, OSA, Box 15.

39. Della Northey to Phineas L. Windsor, 18 November 1912, Northey LSAF.

40. For a fuller account of Anne Hadden's work, see Denise Sallee, "Reconceptualizing Women's History: Anne Hadden and the California Library System," *Libraries & Culture* 27 (Fall 1992): 351–77.

41. Della Northey to Phineas L. Windsor, 18 November 1912, Northey LSAF; Anne Hadden, "Library Trails," *News Notes of California Libraries* (July 1916): 588; and Clara Van Sant to Mary E. Hazeltine, 29 April 1920, WLSP.

42. Harriet Eddy to Mrs. Fred V. Wood, 18 March 1914, Amadin, Fresno, 1908–14, CLFC.

43. Everett R. Perry to Dr. Roberts, 1 July 1912, Marin, Monterey, 1906–14; Librarian, Free Public Library of Santa Barbara, to Dr. Roberts, 29 June 1912, Marin, Monterey, 1906–14; and Sarah E. McCardle to Harriet Eddy, 5 January 1912, Amadin, Fresno, 1908–14, CLFC.

44. Lutie Stearns, "The Experience of a Free-Lance in a Western State," *Bulletin of the American Library Association* 3 (1909): 345.

Chapter 7, pp. 121–133

Epigraph: Mary Frances Isom, Librarian's Report, 1 June 1910, McPL.

1. Mary E. Hazeltine to Dorothy B. Ely, 24 August 1915, Ely LSSR; and Della Northey to Phineas L. Windsor, 7 November 1916, Northey LSAF.

2. Sara Evans, *Born for Liberty* (New York: Free Press, 1989), 173; Roxana Johnson to Frances Simpson, 18 June 1910, Johnson LSAF; and Anne D. Swezey to Frances Simpson, 10 August 1914, Swezey LSAF.

3. Ida A. Kidder to Cornelia Marvin, 25 January 1919, OSA, Box 2.

4. Linda M. Clatworthy, "County Library Experiences," Address given before the Simmons College Library School Class of 1921, Clatworthy Biographical File, DEN.

5. Cornelia Marvin to Mary E. Ahern, 2 April 1925 and 16 April 1928, OSA, Box 2.

6. Mabel Reynolds to Katharine L. Sharp, 3 June 1904, Reynolds LSAF.

7. Ida A. Kidder to Cornelia Marvin, 1 November 1917, OSU, Reel 9; Mabel Reynolds to Katharine L. Sharp, 3 June 1904, Reynolds LSAF;

Della Northey to Frances Simpson, 16 December 1917, Northey SLAF; Anne D. Swezey to Simpson, 10 April 1914, Swezey LSAF; Daisy B. to Marvin, 15 April 1914, OSA, Box 2; and Mabel G. West to Simpson, 31 August 1917, West LSAF.

8. Lucy M. Lewis to Katharine L. Sharp, May 1907, Lewis LSAF; and Lotta Fleek to Mary E. Hazeltine, 29 September 1913, Fleek LSSR.

9. Harriet Bixby to Mary E. Hazeltine, 9 February 1910; and Vera J. Snook to Phineas L. Windsor, 30 March 1925, Snook LSAF.

10. Thomas J. Schlereth, *Victorian America: Transformations in Everyday Life* (New York: HarperCollins, 1991), xv; Maud Osborne to Frances Simpson, 23 September 1911, Osborne LSAF; Ellen Garfield to Mary Frances Isom, 23 January 1908, OSA, Box 2; Mabel Prentiss to J. L. Gillis, 11 November 1905, and Phineas L. Windsor to C. A. Duniway, 16 April 1913, Flora Case LSAF.

11. Alice Lambert to Charlotte A. Baker, 26 August 1915, CAB.

12. "Lo, the Poor Librarian," *The Independent Woman* 1 (January 1920): 4; and Leslie Woodcock Tentler, *Wage-Earning Women: Industrial Work and Family Life in the United States, 1900–1930* (New York: Oxford University Press, 1979), 191, 194.

13. Mabel Reynolds to Frances Simpson, 18 April 1906, Reynolds LSAF; and Belle Sweet to Edna Goss, 9 April 1915, Sweet Letterpress, MBS.

14. Helen V. Calhoun to J. M. Hitt, 9 August 1907, WSL, Box 19; Lotta Fleek to Mary E. Hazeltine, 11 April 1915, Fleek LSSR.

15. Frances Simpson to Margaret Winning, 30 October 1919, Winning LSAF; and William E. Henry to Mary E. Hazeltine, 28 April 1919, WLSP.

16. Charles F. Lummis to M. T. Owens, 7 November 1905, Lummis Papers, SWM.

17. Mary Royce Crawford to Joseph F. Daniels, 18 May 1920, Crawford RAF; and Mabel Reynolds to Katharine L. Sharp, 26 May 1907, Reynolds LSAF.

18. Margaret Eastman to Joseph F. Daniels, 11 February 1920, Eastman RAF.

19. Dorothy B. Ely to Mary E. Hazeltine, 3 August 1915, Ely LSSR; Elizabeth Forrest to Frances Simpson, 29 March 1916, Forrest LSAF; and Theodora Brewitt to Mary E. Hazeltine, 17 March [1911 or 1912], Brewitt LSSR.

20. Mayme Batterson to Anna Price, 9 January 1910, Batterson,

LSAF; Frances Simpson to Clara Abernethy, 30 October 1919, Abernethy LSAF; Simpson to William E. Henry, 23 February 1920, Abernethy LSAF; Corine Kittelson to Mary E. Hazeltine, 24 November 1910, Kittelson LSSR; and Belle Sweet to Edna Goss, 9 April 1915, Sweet Letterpress, MBS.

21. Frances Simpson to Mabel Reynolds, 2 April 1907, Reynolds LSAF; and Mary E. Hazeltine to Mary Egan, 17 July 1916, Egan LSSR.

22. Corine Kittelson to Mary E. Hazeltine, 4 October 1914, LSSR; and Gladys Germand to Hazeltine, 5 December 1915, LSSR.

23. Mary E. Hazeltine to Lena Brownell, 11 April 1919, Brownell LSAF.

24. Florence M. Waller to Frances Simpson, 12 April 1916, Waller LSAF.

25. Lena Brownell to Mary E. Hazeltine, 15 December 1920, LSSR.

26. Wayne A. Wiegand, *"An Active Instrument for Propaganda": The American Public Library During World War I* (New York: Greenwood Press, 1989), 50.

27. *Annual Report of the Spokane Public Library, 1917–1918–1919* (Spokane: Dyer Printing Co., [1919]).

28. Ruth Lewis, [Canon City Library], *Colorado Libraries* 2 (July 1917): 37.

29. Grace Raymond Hebard to Mary E. Hazeltine, 16 September 1918, WLSP; Hebard to Aven Nelson, 26th Annual Report, 26 May 1919, GRH, Box 1; and L. Hamilton to Ernest H. Lindley, 19 July 1918, UG 12, Box 13, Folder 449, University of Idaho.

30. Ferne Ryan Allen, War Department, to Mary E. Hazeltine, September 1918, Allen LSSR; and Ida A. Kidder to Cornelia Marvin, 13 November 1917, 20 July 1916, and 9 May 1918, OSU, Reel 9.

Chapter 8, pp. 135–149

1. Ida A. Kidder LSAF; Myrtle Knepper LSAF; Lucy M. Lewis LSAF; "Field Reports: Ida A. Kidder, 1907– 1908," OSA, Box 7; and Library Correspondence (RG9), OSU.

2. M.E. Kingsbury, "'To Shine in Use': The Library and the War Service of Oregon's Pioneer Librarian, Mary Frances Isom," *Journal of Library History* 10 (1975): 22–34; "Mary Frances Isom," *Dictionary of American Library Biography*, ed. Bohdan S. Wynar (Littleton, CO: Libraries Unlimited, Inc., 1978); and Isom letterpress, Librarian's Reports,

and Board Minutes, Multnomah County Public Library, Portland, Oregon.

3. Charlotte A. Baker Papers, Colorado State University, Fort Collins, Colorado; John Edward Van Male, "A History of Library Extension in Colorado, 1890–1930" (M.A. thesis, University of Denver, 1940); Charlotte A. Baker, "Life as It Comes," *New York State College Alumni Quarterly* 17 (Spring 1936).

4. Belle Sweet Oral History and Sweet letterpress, Special Collections Department, University of Idaho Library; "M. Belle Sweet Passes at 85," *Lewiston* (Idaho) *Tribune*, 30 June 1964; and Sweet LSAF. The Sweet Oral History is transcribed in *The Bookmark* 24/3 (March 1972): 117–22, and 24/4 (June 1972): 151–55.

~ *Bibliography* ~

Primary Sources/Archival and Manuscript Collections

American Library Association Archives, University of Illinois,
    Urbana, Illinois.
        Faxon Photograph Collection
Arizona Department of Library, Archives, and Public Records,
    Phoenix, Arizona.
        Mulford Winsor Papers
California State Archives, Sacramento, California.
        California State Library
            Administrative Correspondence
            Applications for County Librarian, 1911–33
            County Library Files Correspondence
            County Library Organizer Files
        California Library Association Files, 1904–05
Carnegie Library Correspondence, Carnegie Corporation, New York,
    New York.
Colorado State Archives, Denver, Colorado.
        Biennial Reports of the State Board of Library Commissioners
        Biennial Reports of the Superintendent of Public Instruction
Colorado State University Archives, Fort Collins, Colorado.
        Charlotte A. Baker Papers
        Catalogs of the Colorado Agricultural College
        Colorado Agricultural College Bulletins
Columbia University, Rare Book and Manuscript Library, New York,
    New York.
        Melvil Dewey Personal Correspondence
Denver Public Library, Western History Collection, Denver,
    Colorado.
        Denver Public Library Archives
        Denver Public Library Commission Minutes, 1900–1910
        Denver Public Library Training Class, 1911–1931

Charles R. Dudley Papers, 1887–1910
Occasional Leaflet/Colorado Libraries, 1913–1922
Eastern Washington University, Archives, Cheney, Washington.
Annual/Biennial Reports of the Cheney State Normal School
Annual Catalogs
Circulars of Information
General Federation of Women's Clubs, Women's History Resource
Library, Washington, D.C.
Local Club Records
State Federation Records
Idaho State Library, Boise, Idaho.
Biennial Reports of the Free Library Commission of Idaho,
1st (1901–03); 10th (1919–20)
Free Library Commission Correspondence
Indiana State Library, Indianapolis, Indiana.
State Library Correspondence, L971
Los Angeles Public Library, Archives, Los Angeles, California.
Annual Reports
Correspondence
Multnomah County Library, Administrative Archives, Portland,
Oregon.
Board Minutes
Librarian's Reports
Mary Frances Isom Letterpress Volumes
Nebraska State Historical Society, Lincoln, Nebraska.
Nebraska State Library Commission Correspondence
New Mexico State Library, Southwest Room, Santa Fe, New
Mexico.
Clipping File
New Mexico, State Records Center and Archives, Santa Fe, New
Mexico.
Territorial Archives of New Mexico, Microfilm edition
Northwest Room, Spokane Public Library, Spokane, Washington.
Annual Reports, Spokane Public Library, 1914, 1915, 1916,
1917/18/19
Photograph Collection
Oregon Historical Society, Library, Portland, Oregon.
Civic Improvement Association, Carlton, Oregon
Matthew P. Deady Papers

Oregon Federation of Women's Clubs
Walter M. Pierce Papers
Milton W. Smith Papers
Oregon State Archives, Salem, Oregon.
State Library Correspondence, RGL8, 61–8/1 and 61–8/2
Oregon State Library, Salem, Oregon.
Biennial Reports of the Oregon Library Commission
Oregon State University Archives, Corvallis, Oregon.
Library Correspondence, RG9
Ida A. Kidder Biographical File
Riverside City and County Public Library, Special Collections
Department, Riverside, California.
Library Service School Student Records, 1911–21
Southwest Museum, Braun Research Library, Los Angeles,
California.
Charles Lummis Papers
Stanford University, Department of Special Collections, Green
Library, Palo Alto, California.
Annual Reports of the President of the University
Faculty Biographical Files
Library Archives/Correspondence
E. H. Woodruff Papers
University of Colorado, Western Historical Collections, Norlin
Library, Boulder, Colorado.
Colorado Library Association Archives
Colorado University Library Archives
University of Denver, Special Collections Department, Penrose
Library, Denver, Colorado.
Linda M. Clatworthy Biographical File
University of Denver Bulletin
University of Idaho, Department of Special Collections, Moscow,
Idaho.
Barnard-Stockbridge Photograph Collection
James F. Ailshie Papers
President's Office Records, 1893–1965
Mary Belle Sweet Biographical File
Mary Belle Sweet Letterpress Volumes
The University Argonaut
University of Illinois Archives, Urbana, Illinois.

Library School Alumni Files
Library School Director's Office, General Correspondence,
     1905–1962
Katharine L. Sharp Papers
University of Montana, Missoula, Montana.
Gertrude Buckhous Biographical File
University of Northern Colorado, University Archives, Greeley,
Colorado.
Catalogs of the State Normal School of Colorado
Z. X. Snyder Administrative Correspondence
University of Oregon Archives, Eugene, Oregon.
Library Archives (M. Hale Douglass Correspondence)
University of Oregon Catalogs
Walter and Cornelia Marvin Pierce Papers
University of Washington, Manuscripts Department, Washington
University Libraries, Seattle.
Pacific Northwest Library Association Papers
University of Washington, University Archives, Seattle.
Library Directors' Office Records
University of Wisconsin-Madison, University Archives, Madison,
Wisconsin.
Library School Placement Correspondence
Library School Student Records
University of Wyoming, American Heritage Center, Laramie,
Wyoming.
Grace Raymond Hebard Papers
Washington State Archives, Olympia, Washington.
Biennial Reports of the Traveling Library Commission
Washington State Library General Correspondence
Washington State University, Manuscripts, Archives and Special
Collections Department, Holland Library, Pullman, Washington.
Annual Catalogs of the Washington Agricultural College
Library Bulletin
Library Correspondence
Librarian's Report to the President
President E.A. Bryan Correspondence
Wisconsin State Historical Society, Archives, Madison, Wisconsin.
League of Library Commissions Correspondence
Wisconsin Free Library Commission Correspondence

Wyoming State Museum, Historical Research Section, Cheyenne, Wyoming.

  Mabel Wilkinson typescript journal, "Development of the Platte County Free Library, February to June 1915"

Primary Sources/Oral Histories

Interview with Mary Belle Sweet. [n.d.]. Department of Special Collections, University of Idaho, Moscow, Idaho.

Interview with Cornelia Marvin Pierce. 2 January 1956. Oregon Historical Society, Portland, Oregon.

Interview with David C. Duniway. 1981. Oregon Historical Society, Portland, Oregon.

Published Primary Sources/Articles

Ahern, Mary E. "The Business Side of a Woman's Career as a Librarian." *Library Journal* 24 (July 1899): 60–62.

Askew, Sarah. "Library Work in the Open Country." *Annals of the American Academy of Political and Social Science* 67 (1916): 264.

Barnum, Mabel F. "Opportunities for College Women in the Library Profession." *Bostonia* 14 (April 1913): 1–7.

Bowerman, George F. "Libraries." In *International Yearbook: A Compendium of the World's Progress, 900.* New York: Dodd, 1901.

Clark, F. H. "Libraries and Librarians of the Pacific Coast." *The Overland Monthly* 18 (November 1891): 449–64.

Countryman, Gratia. "Librarianship." In *Vocations Open to College Women.* Minneapolis: University of Minnesota, 1913.

Crunden, Frederick. "Fifth Session." *Library Journal* 30 (Conference No. 1905): 168–71.

Cutler, Mary S. "What a Woman Librarian Earns." *Library Journal* 17 (Conference No. 1892): 89–91.

Dana, John Cotton. "The Library Movement in the Far West." *The Library* 8 (1896): 446–50.

Daniels, Joseph F. "Library Work at the State Normal School, Greeley, Colorado." *Public Libraries* 3 (May 1898): 167.

Dewey, Melvil. "Women in Libraries: How They Are Handicapped." *Library Notes* 1 (October 1886): 89–92.

Dockery, Mrs. E.J. "How a Library Commission Was Secured in Idaho." *Library Journal* 26 (Conference No. 1901): 188–90.

Downey, Mary Elizabeth. "Pioneering in Utah." *Bulletin of the American Library Association* 9 (1915): 139–44.

Eddy, Harriet G. "California County Free Libraries." *Bulletin of the American Library Association* 5 (1911): 138–44.

"Facts About Montana Libraries." *Public Libraries* 5 (January 1900): 29.

Fairchild, Salome Cutler. "Women in Libraries." *Library Journal* 29 (December 1904): 157–62.

Foote, Elizabeth L. "Instruction of the Local Librarian by the Organizer." *Public Libraries* 3 (1898): 290–91.

Gillis, J. L. "Co-ordination in Library Work in California." *Bulletin of the American Library Association* 5 (1911): 72–75.

Gladden, George. "The Free Library As a Civilizing Agent." *Outlook* 51 (29 June 1895): 1131–32.

Hadden, Anne. "Library Trails." *News Notes of California Libraries* 11 (January 1916): 581–88.

Haines, Helen E. "The Growth of Traveling Libraries." *World's Work* 8 (September 1904): 5233.

Hayward, Celia A. "Woman as Cataloger." *Public Libraries* 3 (1898): 121–23.

Hazeltine, Mary Emogene. "Opportunities for College Women in Library Work." *The Bookman* (February 1916): 685–91.

Hewins, Caroline M. "Library Work for Women." *Library Journal* 16 (September 1891): 273–74.

Isom, Mary Frances. "County Libraries in Oregon." *Bulletin of the American Library Association* 5 (1911): 144–46.

James, M.S.R. "Women Librarians and Their Future." *Public Libraries* 7 (January 1902): 3–7.

Lummis, Charles F. "Books in Harness." *Out West* 25 (September 1906): 195–225.

———. "The Library Situation in Los Angeles." *Library Journal* 30 (October 1905): 800–802.

Marvin, Cornelia. "Library Commissions and Rural Schools." *Bulletin of the American Library Association* 2 (1908): 314–17.

Mathews, Shailer. "Culture in the West." *World Today* 8 (1904): 191–96.

Putnam, Herbert. "The Prospect: An Address Before a Graduating

Class of Women." *Library Journal* 37 (December 1912): 651–58.

Putnam, Herbert. "What It Means to be a Librarian." *Ladies' Home Journal* 17 (February 1900): 22.

Ralph, Julian. "A Recent Journey Through the West: Modern Library-Work Out West." *Harpers Weekly* 39 (14 September 1895): 871–72.

Rathbone, Josephine Adams. "Salaries of Library School Graduates." *Library Journal* 39 (1914): 188–90.

Richardson, Ernest C. "Modern Library Work: Its Aims and Its Achievements." *The Dial* 38 (1 February 1905): 73–76.

Sharp, Katharine L. "Librarianship as a Profession." *Public Libraries* 3 (January 1898): 5–7.

Shaw, Adele Marie. "The Day's Work of a Librarian." *World's Work* 6 (1903): 3681–86.

Smith, Charles Wesley. "Library Conditions in the Northwest." *Library Journal* 30 (Conference No. 1905): 10–13.

Stearns, Lutie E. "The Experience of a Free Lance in a Western State." *Bulletin of the American Library Association* 3 (1909): 345–48.

Stearns, Lutie E. "How to Organize State Library Commissions and Make State Aid Effective." *Library Journal* 24 (July 1899): 16–18.

"Training Girls for Occupations." *World's Work* 6 (1903): 3815–16.

Tyler, Alice S. "Instructional Work of Library Commissions." *Public Libraries* 10 (February 1905): 60.

Printed Primary Sources/Books and Pamphlets

Buying List of Recent Books Recommended By the Library Commissions of Iowa, Minnesota, Wisconsin, Idaho, Nebraska, and Delaware. Madison: Wisconsin Free Library Commission, 1902.

Colorado Federation of Women's Clubs. *Yearbook.* N.P.: Colorado Federation of Women's Clubs, 1913/14– 1920/21.

Libraries: Their Establishment and Management (Library Laws of Colorado). Denver, Colo.: The Smith-Brooks Printing Co., 1897.

Public Library Handbook, Denver. Denver: The Carson-Harper Co., 1895.

"*Third Annual Report of the Traveling Library Committee of the Colorado Federation of Women's Clubs," Traveling Libraries in Colorado.* N.P.: Colorado Federation of Women's Clubs, October 17, 1902.

Traveling Libraries, Bulletin 40. Albany: University of the State of New York, Home Education Department, 1901.

Secondary Sources/Unpublished Works, Dissertations and M.A. Theses

Clatworthy, Linda M. "Library Survey of Colorado." Master's thesis, University of Denver, 1915.

Fenster, Valmai R. "The University of Wisconsin Library School, A History, 1895–1921." Ph.D. diss., University of Wisconsin-Madison, 1977.

Gorchels, Clarence Clifford. "A Land-Grant University Library: The History of the Library of the Washington State University, 1892–1946." Ph.D. diss., Columbia University, 1971.

Hepworth, Bobbie McGee. "Carnegie Libraries in Utah." Master's thesis, Brigham Young University, 1976.

Martinson, Sandra. "The University, the Library, and Miss Sweet: History of the University of Idaho Library, 1892–1948." November 1963. Unpublished typescript, Department of Special Collections, University of Idaho, Moscow, Idaho.

Van Male, John Edward. "A History of Library Extension in Colorado, 1890–1930." Master's thesis, University of Denver, 1940.

Van Slyck, Abigail Ayers. "Free to All: Carnegie Libraries and the Transformation of American Culture, 1886–1917." Ph.D. diss., University of California, Berkeley, 1989.

Secondary Sources/Articles

Antler, Joyce. "After College, What?: New Graduates and the Family Claim." *American Quarterly* 32 (Fall 1980): 409–34.

Bauman, Paula M. "Single Women Homesteaders in Wyoming, 1880–1930." *Annals of Wyoming* 58 (Spring 1986): 39–49.

Bernard, Richard M. and Maris Vinovskis. "The Female School Teacher in Antebellum Massachusetts." *Journal of Social History* 10 (1977): 332–45.

Brisley, Melissa Ann. "Cornelia Marvin Pierce: Pioneer in Library Extension." *Library Quarterly* 38 (April 1968): 125–53.

Brumburg, Joan Jacobs and Nancy Tomes. "Women in the Professions: A Research Agenda for American Historians." *Reviews in American History* 10 (June 1982): 275–96.

Butchart, Ronald E. "The Frontier Teacher: Arizona, 1875–1925." *Journal of the West* 16 (March 1977): 545–66.

Cookingham, Mary E. "Combining Marriage, Motherhood, and Jobs Before World War II: Women College Graduates, Classes of 1905–1935." *Journal of Family History* 9 (Summer 1984): 178–95.

de Graaf, Lawrence B. "Race, Sex, and Region: Black Women in the American West, 1850–1920." *Pacific Historical Review* 49 (May 1980): 285–313.

Faragher, John Mack. "History from the Inside Out: Writing the History of Women in Rural America." *American Quarterly* 33 (1981): 537–57.

Goldin, Claudia. "The Work and Wages of Single Women, 1870 to 1920." *Journal of Economic History* 40 (March 1980): 81–88.

Hanson, Mary Ellen and Carl A. Hanson. "Wilma Loy Shelton: Library Leader in New Mexico, 1920–1950." *New Mexico Historical Review* 64 (January 1989): 51–76.

Hildenbrand, Suzanne. "A Historical Perspective on Gender Issues in American Librarianship." *The Canadian Journal of Information Science* 17 (September 1992): 18–27.

_____. "Some Theoretical Considerations on Women in Library History." *Journal of Library History* 18 (1983): 382–90.

Hoyt, Mary E. "The Colorado School of Mines Library." *Mines Magazine* 26 (1936): 16–17.

Hurst, Lannie. "Ina Coolbrith: Forgotten as Poet . . . Remembered as Librarian." *PNLA Quarterly* 41 (Summer 1977): 4–11.

Jameson, Elizabeth. "Towards a Multicultural History of Women in the Western United States." *Signs: Journal of Women in Culture and Society* 13 (Summer 1988): 761–91.

_____. "Women as Workers, Women as Civilizers: True Womanhood in the American West." In *The Women's West*, edited by Susan Armitage and Elizabeth Jameson. Norman: University of Oklahoma Press, 1987.

Jones, W. "Wyoming's Carnegie Libraries." *Wyoming Library Roundup* 32 (March 1977): 12.

Kaufman, Polly W. "The Library in American Culture." *History of Education Quarterly* 23 (1983): 83–89.

_____. "A Wider Field of Usefulness: Pioneer Women Teachers in the West, 1848–1854." *Journal of the West* 21 (April 1982): 16–25.

Kryder, LeeAnne G. "Self-Assertion and Social Commitment: The Significance of Work to the Progressive Era's New Woman." *Journal of American Culture* 6 (Summer 1983): 25–30.

Maack, Mary Niles. "Toward a History of Women in Librarianship: A Critical Analysis With Suggestions for Further Research." *Journal of Library History* 17 (Spring 1982): 164–85.

McMullen, Haynes, "The Prevalence of Libraries in the Middle West and Far West Before 1876." *Libraries & Culture* 26 (Spring 1991): 441–63.

Manning, Leslie A., guest editor, special issue. *The Journal of the West* 30 (July 1991).

Nelson, Gail K. and John V. Richardson. "Adelaide Hasse and the Early History of the U.S. Superintendent of Documents Classification Scheme." *Government Publications Review* 13 (January/February 1986): 79–96.

Palmieri, Patricia A. "Patterns of Achievement of Single Academic Women at Wellesley College, 1880–1920." *Frontiers* 5 (Spring 1980): 63–67.

Pascoe, Peggy. "Western Women at the Cultural Crossroads." In *Trails: Toward a New Western History,* edited by Patricia Nelson Limerick, Clyde A. Milner II, and Charles E. Rankin. Lawrence: University Press of Kansas, 1991.

Passet, Joanne E. "'Order is Heaven's First Law': Itinerant Librarians and Bibliographic Control, 1887–1915." *Library Quarterly* 60 (January 1990): 23–43.

_____. "Women Academic Librarians on the Western Frontier, 1900–1920." *Library Quarterly* 60 (1990): 320–36.

Petty, Mary E. "Trailblazing Librarians: The Women Who Founded the Spokane Mountaineers." *Alki: The Washington Library Journal* 8 (December 1992): 23–25.

Rankin, Charles E. "Teaching: Opportunity and Limitation for Wyoming Women." *Western Historical Quarterly* (May 1990): 147–70.

Rosenberg, Rosalind. "The Limits of Access: The History of Coeducation in America." In *Women and Higher Education in America,* edited by John Mack Faragher and Florence Howe. New York: Norton, 1988.

Sallee, Denise. "Reconceptualizing Women's History: Anne Hadden and the California County Library System." *Libraries & Culture* 27 (Fall 1992): 351–77.

Scharff, Virginia. "The Independent and Feminine Life: Grace Raymond Hebard, 1861–1936." In *Lone Voyagers: Academic Women in Coeducational Institutions, 1870–1937*, edited by Geraldine Joncich Clifford. New York: The Feminist Press, 1989.

Schierling, Ingrid, editor and Colorado Library Association Centennial Committee Chair, special issue. *Colorado Libraries* 18 (September 1992).

Sicherman, Barbara. "Reading and Ambition: M. Carey Thomas and Female Heroism." *American Quarterly* 45 (March 1993): 73–103.

_____. "Sense and Sensibility: A Case Study of Women's Reading in Later Victorian America." In *Reading in America: Literature and Social History*, edited by Cathy Davidson. Baltimore: Johns Hopkins University Press, 1989.

Underwood, June O. "Civilizing Kansas: Women's Organizations, 1880–1920." *Kansas History* 7 (Winter 1984/85): 291–306.

Underwood, Kathleen. "The Pace of Their Own Lives: Teacher Training and the Life Course of Western Women." *Pacific Historical Review* 55 (November 1986): 513–30.

Wiegand, Wayne A. "Lion and the Lady Revisited: Another Look at the Firing of Mary L. Jones as Los Angeles Public Librarian in 1905." *Library and Information Science Research* 5 (Fall 1983): 273–90.

_____. "Oregon's Public Libraries During the First World War." *Oregon Historical Quarterly* 90 (Spring 1989): 39–63.

Secondary Sources/Books and Pamphlets

Abbott, Andrew D. *The System of Professions: An Essay on the Division of Expert Labor*. Chicago: University of Chicago Press, 1988.

Aptheker, Bettina. *Tapestries of Life: Women's Work, Women's Consciousness and the Meaning of Daily Experience*. Amherst: University of Massachusetts Press, 1989.

Armitage, Susan and Elizabeth Jameson, eds. *The Women's West*. Norman: University of Oklahoma Press, 1987.

Aron, Cindy Sondik. *Ladies and Gentlemen of the Civil Service: Middle-Class Workers in Victorian America*. New York: Oxford University Press, 1987.

Benson, Susan Porter. *Counter Cultures: Saleswomen, Managers, and Customers in American Department Stores, 1890–1940.* Urbana: University of Illinois Press, 1986.

Bernard, Jesse. *Academic Women.* University Park: Pennsylvania State University Press, 1964.

Billington, Ray Allen. *The Far Western Frontier, 1830– 1960.* New York: Harper, 1956.

Blair, Karen J. *The Clubwoman as Feminist: True Womanhood Redefined, 1868–1914.* New York: Holmes & Meier Publishers, 1980.

_____. *Women in the Pacific Northwest: An Anthology.* Seattle: University of Washington Press, 1988.

Bobinski, George S. *Carnegie Libraries: Their History and Impact on American Public Library Development.* Chicago: American Library Association, 1969.

Bosworth, Louise M. *The Living Wage of Women Workers.* Boston: Longmans, Green, and Co., 1911.

Breckinridge, Sophonisba P. *Women in the Twentieth Century.* New York: McGraw Hill, 1933.

Breed, Clara E. *Turning the Pages: San Diego Public Library History, 1882–1982.* San Diego: Friends of the San Diego Public Library, 1983.

Brown, Dee. *The Gentle Tamers: Women of the Old Wild West.* New York: Putnam, 1958.

Burke, John. *The Legend of Baby Doe: The Life and Times of the Silver Queen of the West.* Lincoln: University of Nebraska Press, 1974.

Butler, Anne M. *Daughters of Joy, Sisters of Misery: Prostitutes in the American West, 1865–90.* Urbana: University of Illinois Press, 1985.

Carlson, William H. *The Library of Oregon State University: Its Origins, Management, and Growth.* Corvallis, Oregon: Oregon State University, 1966.

Chafe, William H. *The Paradox of Change: American Women in the 20th Century.* New York: Oxford University Press, 1991.

Chamberlain, Ralph V. *The University of Utah: A History of Its First Hundred Years, 1850 to 1950.* Salt Lake City: University of Utah Press, 1960.

Clifford, Geraldine Joncich, ed. *The Lone Voyagers: Academic Women in Coeducational Institutions, 1870–1937.* New York: The Feminist Press, 1989.

Cordier, Mary Hurlbut. *Schoolwomen of the Prairies and Plains: Personal Narratives from Iowa, Kansas, and Nebraska, 1860s to 1920s.* Albuquerque: University of New Mexico Press, 1992.

Cott, Nancy F. *The Grounding of Modern Feminism.* New Haven, Conn.: Yale University Press, 1987.

Croly, Jane C. *The History of the Women's Club Movement in America.* New York: H. G. Allen & Co., 1898.

Cronon, William, George Miles, and Jay Gitlin, eds. *Under an Open Sky: Rethinking America's Western Past.* New York: W. W. Norton and Company, 1992.

Crunden, Robert M. *Ministers of Reform: The Progressives' Achievement in American Civilization, 1889–1920.* Urbana: University of Illinois Press, 1984.

Davies, Marjorie W. *Woman's Place is at the Typewriter: Office Work and Office Workers, 1870–1930.* Philadelphia: Temple University Press, 1983.

Davis, Donald G. and John M. Tucker, eds. *American Library History: A Comprehensive Guide to the Literature.* Santa Barbara, Calif.: ABC-CLIO, Inc., 1989.

Deutsch, Sarah. *No Separate Refuge: Culture, Class, and Gender on an Anglo-Hispanic Frontier in the American Southwest, 1880–1940.* New York: Oxford University Press, 1987.

Doten, Samuel B. *An Illustrated History of the University of Nevada.* Reno: University of Nevada, 1924.

Eddy, Harriet G. *County Free Library Organizing in California, 1909–18: Personal Recollections.* Berkeley: California Library Association, 1955.

Evans, Sara. *Born for Liberty: A History of Women in America.* New York: The Free Press, 1989.

Faragher, John M. *Women and Men on the Overland Trail.* New Haven: Yale University Press, 1979.

Fink, Deborah. *Agrarian Women: Wives and Mothers in Rural Nebraska, 1880–1940.* Chapel Hill: University of North Carolina Press, 1992.

Fischer, Christiane, ed. *Let Them Speak for Themselves: Women in the American West, 1849–1900.* Hamden, Conn.: Archon Books, 1977.

Garrison, Dee. *Apostles of Culture: The Public Librarian and American Society, 1876–1920.* New York: The Free Press, 1979.

Gates, Charles M. *The First Century at the University of Washington, 1861–1961.* Seattle: University of Washington Press, 1961.

Geller, Evelyn. *Forbidden Books in American Public Libraries,*
1876–1939: A Study in Cultural Change. Westport, Conn.:
Greenwood, 1984.

Gibbs, Rafe. *Beacon for Mountain and Plain: Story of the University of*
Idaho. Moscow: University of Idaho, 1962.

Glazer, Penina M. and Miriam Slater. *Unequal Colleagues: The Entrance*
of Women into the Professions, 1890–1940. New Brunswick: Rutgers
University Press, 1987.

Goldman, Marion S. *Gold Diggers and Silver Miners: Prostitution and*
Social Life on the Comstock Lode. Ann Arbor: University of Michigan
Press, 1981.

Gordon, Lynn D. *Gender and Higher Education in the Progressive Era.*
New Haven, Conn.: Yale University Press, 1990.

Green, Harvey. *The Uncertainty of Everyday Life, 1915– 45.* New York:
HarperCollins, 1992.

Grotzinger, Laurel A. *The Power and the Dignity: Librarianship and*
Katharine Sharp. New York: Scarecrow Press, 1966.

Haber, Samuel. *The Quest for Authority and Honor in the American*
Professions, 1750–1900. Chicago: University of Chicago Press,
1991.

Hardy, Deborah. *Wyoming University: The First 100 Years, 1886–1986.*
Laramie: University of Wyoming, 1986.

Hatch, Nathan O., ed. *The Professions in American History.* Notre
Dame, Ind.: University of Notre Dame Press, 1988.

Haywood, C. Robert. *Victorian West: Class & Culture in Kansas Cattle*
Towns. Lawrence: University Press of Kansas, 1991.

Heim, Kathleen, ed. *The Status of Women in Librarianship: Historical,*
Sociological and Economic Issues. New York: Neal-Schuman, 1983.

Held, Raymond E. *The Rise of the Public Library in California.* Chicago:
American Library Association, 1973.

Hill, H. W., ed. *The Semicentennial Celebration of the Founding of the*
University of Southern California, 1880–1930. Los Angeles: University
of Southern California Press, 1930.

Hill, Joseph A. *Women in Gainful Occupation, 1870–1920.* Census
Monograph No. 9. Washington, D.C.: Government Printing
Office, 1929.

Hine, Robert V. *Community on the American Frontier: Separate But Not*
Alone. Norman: University of Oklahoma Press, 1990.

Hoffman, Nancy. *Woman's "True" Profession: Voices from the History of Education*. Old Westbury, N.Y.: The Feminist Press, 1981.

Hoglund, Elizabeth, ed. *Remembering the University of Utah*. Salt Lake City: University of Utah Press, 1981.

Hopkins, Ernest J. and Alfred Thomas, Jr. *The Arizona State University Story*. Phoenix: Southwest Publishing Co., Inc. 1960.

Jeffrey, Julie Roy. *Frontier Women: The Trans-Mississippi West, 1840–1880*. New York: Hill and Wang, 1979.

Kaufman, Polly Welts. *Women Teachers on the Frontier*. New Haven: Yale University Press, 1984.

Kropp, Simon F. *That All May Learn: New Mexico State University, 1888–1964*. Las Cruces: New Mexico State University, 1972.

Larson, Magali Sarfatti. *The Rise of Professionalism: A Sociological Analysis*. Berkeley: The University of California Press, 1977.

Lich, Glen E., ed. *Regional Studies: The Interplay of Land and People*. College Station: Texas A & M University Press, 1992.

Limerick, Patricia Nelson. *The Legacy of Conquest: The Unbroken Past of the American West*. New York: W. W. Norton, 1987.

Limerick, Patricia Nelson, Clyde A. Milner, and Charles E. Rankin, eds. *Trails: Toward a New Western History*. Lawrence: University Press of Kansas, 1991.

McCarthy, Kathleen D. *Lady Bountiful Revisited: Women, Philanthropy, and Power*. New Brunswick: Rutgers University Press, 1990.

_____. *Women's Culture: American Philanthropy and Art, 1830–1930*. Chicago: University of Chicago Press, 1991.

Malone, Michael P., ed. *Historians and the American West*. Lincoln: University of Nebraska Press, 1983.

Malone, Michael P. and Richard W. Etulain. *The American West: A Twentieth-century History*. Lincoln: University of Nebraska Press, 1989.

Martin, Douglas De Veny. *The Lamp in the Desert: The Story of the University of Arizona*. Tucson: University of Arizona Press, 1960.

Martin, Theodora Penny. *The Sound of Our Own Voices: Women's Study Clubs, 1860–1910*. Boston: Beacon Press, 1987.

Melosh, Barbara. *The Physician's Hand: Work, Culture, and Conflict in American Nursing*. Philadelphia: Temple University Press, 1982.

Meyerowitz, Joanne J. *Women Adrift: Independent Wage Earners in Chicago, 1880–1930*. Chicago: University of Chicago Press, 1988.

Moldow, Gloria. *Women Doctors in Gilded-Age Washington: Race, Gender, and Professionalization.* Urbana: University of Illinois Press, 1987.

Moynihan, Ruth B., Susan Armitage, and Christine Fischer Dichamp. *So Much to Be Done: Women Settlers on the Mining and Ranching Frontier.* Nebraska: University of Nebraska, 1990.

Myres, Sandra L. *Westering Women and the Frontier Experience, 1800–1915.* Albuquerque: University of New Mexico Press, 1982.

_____, ed. *Ho for California!: Women's Overland Diaries from the Huntington Library.* San Marino: Huntington Library, 1980.

Nelson, Paula. *After the West Was Won: Homesteaders and Townbuilders in Western South Dakota, 1900–1917.* Iowa City: University of Iowa Press, 1986.

Newcomer, Mabel. *A Century of Higher Education for American Women.* New York: Harper, 1959.

Nichols, Roger L., ed. *American Frontier and Western Issues: A Historiographical Review.* New York: Greenwood Press, 1986.

Norton, Justin. *So Sweet to Labor: Rural Women in America, 1865–1895.* New York: Viking Press, 1979.

Pascoe, Peggy. *Relations of Rescue.* New York: Oxford University Press, 1990.

Peiss, Kathy. *Cheap Amusements: Working Women and Leisure in Turn-of-the-Century New York.* Philadelphia: Temple University Pres, 1986.

Peterson, Kenneth G. *The University of California Library at Berkeley, 1900–1945.* Berkeley: University of California Press, 1970.

Petrik, Paula. *No Step Backward: Women and Family on the Rocky Mountain Frontier, Helena, Montana, 1865–1900.* Helena: Montana Historical Society Press, 1987.

Poling-Kemp, Lesley. *The Harvey Girls: Women Who Opened the West.* New York: Paragon House, 1989.

Reverby, Susan M. *Ordered to Care: The Dilemma of American Nursing, 1850–1945.* New York: Cambridge University Press, 1987.

Riley, Glenda. *The Female Frontier: A Comparative View of Women on the Prairie and the Plains.* Lawrence: University Press of Kansas, 1988.

Robertson, Janet. *The Magnificent Mountain Women: Adventure in the Colorado Rockies.* Lincoln: University of Nebraska Press, 1990.

Rosenberg, Rosalind. *Divided Lives: American Women in the Twentieth Century.* New York: Hill and Wang, 1992.

Rossiter, Margaret W. *Women Scientists in America: Struggles and Strategies to 1940.* Baltimore: The Johns Hopkins University Press, 1982.

Scadron, Arlene, ed. *On Their Own: Widows and Widowhood in the American Southwest, 1848–1939.* Urbana: University of Illinois Press, 1988.

Schackel, Sandra. *Social Housekeepers: Women Shaping Public Policy in New Mexico, 1920–1940.* Albuquerque: University of New Mexico Press, 1992.

Schlereth, Thomas. *Victorian America: Transformations in Everyday Life, 1876–1915.* New York: HarperCollins, 1991.

Schlissel, Lillian. *Women's Diaries of the Westward Journey.* New York: Schocken Books, 1982.

Schlissel, Lillian, Byrd Gibbens, and Elizabeth Hampsten. *Far From Home: Families of the Westward Journey.* New York: Schocken Books, 1989.

Schlissel, Lillian, Vicki L. Ruiz, and Janice Monk, eds. *Western Women: Their Land, Their Lives.* Albuquerque: University of New Mexico Press, 1988.

Scott, Anne Firor. *Natural Allies: Women's Associations in American History.* Urbana: University of Illinois, 1991.

Shiflett, Orvin Lee. *Origins of American Academic Librarianship.* Norwood, N.J.: Ablex, 1989.

Solomon, Barbara Miller. *In the Company of Educated Women.* New Haven: Yale University Press, 1985.

The Status of Women in Librarianship: Historical, Sociological and Economic Issues. Ed. by Kathleen Heim. New York: Neal-Schuman, 1983.

Stegner, Wallace. *The Gathering of Zion: The Story of the Mormon Trail.* New York: McGraw-Hill, 1964.

Steward, George R. *The California Trail: An Epic with Many Heroes.* New York: McGraw-Hill, 1962.

Stratton, Joanna L. *Pioneer Women: Voices from the Kansas Frontier.* New York: Simon and Schuster, 1981.

Turner, Frederick Jackson. *The Significance of the Frontier in American History.* Madison: State Historical Society of Wisconsin, 1984.

Underwood, Kathleen. *Town Building on the Colorado Frontier.* Albuquerque: University of New Mexico Press, 1987.

Unruh, John D., Jr. *The Plains Across: The Overland Emigrants and the Trans-Mississippi West, 1840–60.* Urbana: University of Illinois, 1979.

Vann, Sarah K. *Training for Librarianship Before 1923.* Chicago: American Library Association, 1961.

Vicinus, Martha. *Independent Women: Work and Community for Single Women, 1850–1920*. Chicago: University of Chicago Press, 1985.

Wade, Richard C. *The Urban Frontier: The Rise of Western Cities, 1790–1830*. Cambridge: Harvard University Press, 1959.

Warren, Donald E., ed. *American Teachers: Histories of a Profession at Work*. New York: Macmillan, 1989.

Weiner, Lynn Y. *From Working Girl to Working Mother: The Female Labor Force in the United States, 1820–1980*. Chapel Hill: University of North Carolina Press, 1985.

White, Carl M. *A Historical Introduction to Library Education: Problems and Progress to 1951*. Metuchen, N.J.: Scarecrow Press, 1976.

White, Richard, *"It's Your Misfortune and None of My Own": A History of the American West* (Norman: University of Oklahoma Press, 1991.

Wiegand, Wayne A. *"An Active Instrument for Propaganda": The American Public Library During World War I*. New York: Greenwood Press, 1989.

Williamson, Charles C. *Training for Library Work*. Reprinted in *The Williamson Reports of 1921 and 1923*. Metuchen, N.J.: Scarecrow Press, 1971.

Wilson, Margaret Gibbons. *The American Woman in Transition: The Urban Influence, 1870–1920*. Westport, Conn.: Greenwood Press, 1979.

Young, Arthur P. *Books for Sammies: The American Library Association and World War I*. Pittsburgh: Beta Phi Mu, 1981.

Zumberge, James Herbert. *The University of Southern California: Centennial Retrospective*. New York: Newcomen Society of North America, 1981.

Secondary Sources/Journals

Bulletin of the American Library Association
LAPL Monthly Bulletin
Library Journal
News Notes of California Libraries
Occasional Leaflet [Colorado Library Association]
Proceedings: Pacific Northwest Library Association
Public Libraries

Index

Mechanical work, see Clerical work
Medford, Oregon, 119
Mill Valley, California, 106
Mills College, 67
Ministers, support of libraries, 95, 97–98
Mission, sense of, xiv, 64, 72–73, 75, 81–82, 122, 139
Mitchell, Mary Grenning, 84
Modesto, California, 11, 85
Montana State College of Agriculture and Mechanical Arts, 59, 62, 66, 68–69, 73
Montana, University of, 57, 67, 74
Monterey, California, 10, 44, 98, 119
Monterey Library Association, 10
Morgan, Edith, 52, 57, 60, 73–74
Mormons, see Latter-day Saints
Moscow, Idaho, 43–46, 51 (illus.)

Native Americans, xiii; Library service to, 115
Nevada, Library Development in, 90
New Mexico College of Agriculture and Mechanic Arts, 52, 61 (illus.), 63–64, 68, 144–45
New York State Library School, 23
Newcastle, California, 100
Normal School Libraries, see Academic libraries
Northey, Della, 118
Nursing, professionalization of, 4

Occasional Leaflet, 146
One-person libraries, 56, 129
Oregon Library Association, 141
Oregon State Agricultural College, 47, 66–68, 74, 132, 137, 139
Oregon State Federation of Women's Clubs, 79, 142
Oregon State Library Commission, 79–80, 137
Oregon, University of, 74
Orphans, French, 132

Pacific Northwest Library Association, 57, 141
Package libraries, 73
Parmalee Traveling Library Company, 99
Pendleton, Oregon, 43, 50, 105, 107, 116

Perry, Everett R., 119
Pests, 69–70
Pike's Peak, 41
Placerville, California, 12
Playgrounds, 111
Platte County, Wyoming, 91–94, 113
Politics, in colleges, universities, and normal schools, 63
Pomona College, 67
Portland, Oregon, 14, 35, 41, 79–80
Pratt Institute Library School, 141
Prentiss, Mabel, 50, 90, 95–101
Progressive era woman/women, xiv, 2, 21
Progressives, definition of, 17–18
Public Libraries, Absence of, 73; during World War I, 130; in Oregon, 10; Opposition to, 13, 98–100, 199; Outreach, 111, 114
Public Library of Portland, 33, 45, 55–56, 112, 115; see also Library Association of Portland
Pullman, Washington, 41–43, 47

Qualifications sought in librarians, 105

Railroads, 42
Rankin, Jeannette, 30
Rathbone, Josephine Adams, 141
Raton, New Mexico, Public Library, 108 (illus.), 109 (illus.)
Reading, and the literary canon, 114–16; benefits of, 22, 85–87
Reading interests of library school students, 21–22, 25; of women, 21, of western residents, 88
Religious affiliation of librarians, 105
Reynolds, Mabel, 72, 127, 129
Richardson, Ernest C., 79
Ridenbaugh Hall, 47; 48, 49 (illus.)
Ritchie, Elizabeth, 57
Ritzville, Washington, 106
Riverside Public Library, School of Library Service, xviii, 22–23; 32
Rocklin, California, 98
Rural communities, Life in, 49, 52, 54
Rural residents, library service to, 73, 117–19; interest in traveling libraries, 94